Praise for *Now You're Thinking!*

"Your mind is your most powerful tool. This book can help you chart a course for sharpening your critical thinking skills so you can make better decisions in all areas of life."

—**Daniel H. Pink**, author of *Drive* and *A Whole New Mind*

"Critical thinking is the #1 skill required to build the workforce of tomorrow. *Now You're Thinking!* is a valuable and very *useful* book that provides the tools and techniques required to make better decisions. With a heart-lifting and inspiring true story, this book guides you through the process of becoming an extraordinary thinker. This one delivers!"

—**Ed Reilly**, President and CEO, American Management Association, International

"While writing *The Speed of Trust* it became clear to us that people would not trust others to lead them if they did not trust their thinking. If you read and apply the principles in this book, people will come to see you as a leader."

—**Stephen M. R. Covey**, author of *The New York Times* and #1 *Wall Street Journal* bestseller, *The Speed of Trust*

"A big part of being a leader is making decisions—but how often do we stop and think about our own decision-making processes? Using the unique backdrop of a real-life military, medical, and civilian team that effectively combined their intellect and courage to save a young Iraqi child's life, the authors illustrate a five-step model we can all use to more effectively process our own thoughts toward successful decisions. This book is a must-read."

—**Ken Blanchard**, coauthor of *The One Minute Manager*® and *Full Steam Ahead!*

"If you are striving to be better, faster, and different in life, to have more fulfillment and success, you need this book. A great primer to increase and enhance your thinking skills and processes."

—**Harry Paul**, coauthor of *FISH! A Proven Way to Boost Morale and Improve Results*

"*Now You're Thinking!* will transform your thinking—and change your life!"

—**Marshall Goldsmith**, author of *The New York Times* bestsellers, *MOJO* and *What Got You Here Won't Get You There*

"With today's shortened attention spans, texting, blogging, and instant gratification, the rational thinking skills in *Now You're Thinking!* are more pertinent than ever. In the workplace, quick reactions and assumptions have resulted in industrial accidents. As a Navy veteran and lifelong learner, I believe this book has arrived at a critical time."

—**Mike Miller**, Vice President, Technology Transfer Services, Inc.

"We are currently going through a major upheaval that is impacting all of our lives. We can choose to be 'masters of our fate' or simply get swept along by the tides of change. If the choice is the former, a substantial upgrade of our critical thinking skills will be required.

"*Now You're Thinking!* is a rewarding and understandable read. No matter how successful you may be, this book will sharpen your decision-making skills. For those who may question their abilities, you will find the thinking exercises practical and usable.

"You will be richer for the reading."

—**Arne Carlson**, Governor of Minnesota (1991–1999)

"This is a powerful book with a great message. It challenges the prevailing view that thinking skills can't be developed, and it provides useful and practical guidance on how someone can improve the quality and effectiveness of their thinking."

—**Stuart S. Crandell**, Senior Vice President, Global Solutions, PDI Ninth House

"Most people come and go in Hollywood. Some stay, become icons, and enjoy lasting success. These are the ones who think differently. This is a book about how to think differently and how you can enjoy lasting success for yourself. It is also a great read."

—**Rob Guralnick**, former Executive Vice President, Production, Warner Brothers

"With its focus on enhancing critical thinking, *Now You're Thinking!* is well timed to help students meet contemporary global challenges. Intensified labor competition requires improved intellectual preparation within a fully informed academic environment, and professors can respond with the tools offered within *Now You're Thinking!* Everybody gains from the skills *Now You're Thinking!* pinpoints. The more widely utilized this book becomes, the more the benefits will be widely distributed.

"This is a book where everyone wins."

—**Marcus Breen**, Ph.D., Professor and Head of School, Communication, and Media, Bond University, Gold Coast, Queensland, Australia

"*Now You're Thinking!* uses a compelling, real-life experience to highlight the tools each of us needs to become a better thinker. This book is a must-read for students of all ages!"

—**Bob Hipp**, President, Pennridge Community Education Foundation, www.pennridgefoundation.org

Now You're Thinking

Now You're Thinking

Change Your Thinking...
Transform Your Life

Judy Chartrand
Stewart Emery
Russ Hall
Heather Ishikawa
John Maketa

Vice President, Publisher: Tim Moore
Associate Publisher and Director of Marketing: Amy Neidlinger
Editorial Assistant: Pamela Boland
Senior Marketing Manager: Julie Phifer
Assistant Marketing Manager: Megan Graue
Cover Designer: Alan Clements
Managing Editor: Kristy Hart
Project Editor: Betsy Harris
Copy Editor: Karen Annett
Proofreader: Sheri Cain
Senior Indexer: Cheryl Lenser
Interior Designer: Nonie Ratcliff
Compositor: Nonie Ratcliff
Manufacturing Buyer: Dan Uhrig

© 2012 by Pearson Education, Inc.
Publishing as FT Press
Upper Saddle River, New Jersey 07458

FT Press offers excellent discounts on this book when ordered in quantity for bulk
purchases or special sales. For more information, please contact U.S. Corporate and
Government Sales, 1-800-382-3419, corpsales@pearsontechgroup.com. For sales outside
the U.S., please contact International Sales at international@pearson.com.

Third Printing May 2012

ISBN-10: 0-13-269013-6
ISBN-13: 978-0-13-269013-3

Pearson Education LTD.
Pearson Education Australia PTY, Limited.
Pearson Education Singapore, Pte. Ltd.
Pearson Education Asia, Ltd.
Pearson Education Canada, Ltd.
Pearson Educación de Mexico, S.A. de C.V.
Pearson Education—Japan
Pearson Education Malaysia, Pte. Ltd.

Library of Congress Library of Congress Cataloging-in-Publication Data

Now you're thinking : change your thinking— transform your life
/ Judy Chartrand ... [et al.].
    p. cm.
  ISBN 978-0-13-269013-3 (hbk. : alk. paper)
  1. Critical thinking. 2. Problem solving. 3. Decision making. I. Chartrand, Judy Marie.
BF441.N69 2012
  153.4'2—dc22
                        2011012752

*Dedicated to the men and women of the armed forces
at home and abroad, with thanks for their commitment
and sacrifices... and their sound and careful thinking
in trying situations.*

Contents

Foreword

It has taken me a long time to understand that creating success in your life, and maximizing your potential, is about knowing who you are. This takes being clear about what your values are and what deeply matters to you. It involves knowing what you are passionate about, what you love to do, and developing your talent, skills, and abilities. It means knowing that you first have to get good before you can become great as you work to develop your talent and build your skills.

As you put these pieces together, you establish your identity. This matters because your identity is your passport to freedom. However, your identity has to be *your* identity. There are a lot of folks out there trying to tell you what should matter to you, what you should care about, what you should be when you grow up (no matter what your age!), along with how you should get there and what you should wear for the journey.

With the expansion of global opportunities and the explosion of technology, we are inundated with so many opportunities to think that we have to be like somebody else without realizing that being ourselves is where our influence and opportunity to grow really lies.

It is very difficult to be yourself today if you get stuck in a box with a label. You end up doing the same things over and over every day, often for the rest of your life. The missing piece is we may never think about how to take the education we have, the information available to us, and make it relevant to our identity and who we are. Additionally, the educational system teaches us to memorize, take tests, repeat back information and labels us with a grade—and all while we forget most of what we learned. So what is the missing piece in most of our lives? We forget how to think. We forget how to take information and make it relevant to growing and developing our lives in the 24 hours that we have every day—which is the only thing that makes us all equal. Everybody has 24 hours.

True happiness is about doing things that we love and doing things that we want to be successful at. This starts with building from the inside out, as opposed to having the world define us, when we should be working on defining ourselves. We are often programmed to believe that the labels we are given are ours. We often can't get past our environment, we can't get past our circumstances, we can't get beyond our race or gender or our parental programming. If we buy into all these external forces and addictions, we will never find our core and we will miss building our authentic lives. We may look great on the outside and we all have the moves down, but we will be empty on the inside. And we will never reach our God-given natural potential as human beings.

All that we're talking about here takes some work and sacrifice. We have to pay attention to our own experience. We have to learn to integrate our mind, body, spirit, and emotions so we can live in the world authentically and be engaged. We have to work to become comfortable in our own skin. We have to work to consistently define ourselves as opposed to having other people define us. This is the process for innovation and creativity. When we do this, people will describe us as people who know who we are. They will say that we are comfortable in our own skin. They will like themselves more when they are in our presence.

In our world today, it is important to learn the art of critical thinking. It takes critical thinking to cut through the noise of other people's opinions swirling around you like the fog of darkness threatening to engulf your soul. Surrounded by pundits and pitch-men purveying mostly ungrounded assertions, you need a disci-plined thought style to establish your own authentic identity. Sifting through experiences for the dream of a future uniquely yours is a task for critical thinking and development. When every-body has access to an avalanche of information, becoming a mas-ter thinker is very important in your life-long security.

You can master the art of thinking. This book can be your guide and show you how.

—Stedman Graham
Author, Educator, and Entrepreneur

Acknowledgments

The authors wish to thank all the participants in the story for sharing their time and memories. We also thank the folks at the FT Press for their support and encouragement: Megan Colvin, Betsy Harris, Timothy C. Moore, and Amy Neidlinger, as well as Karen Chiang, Chad Fife, Ray Blom, John Trent, and Breanne Potter-Harris from the Pearson TalentLens Group.

About the Authors

Judy Chartrand is a recognized thought leader in the areas of critical thinking and career development. Chartrand works as a consulting Chief Scientist with Pearson. As a psychologist, Chartrand has helped hundreds of clients increase their personal and career satisfaction. She frequently speaks at national and international conferences and has published more than 50 articles and books. Chartrand lives in Minnesota with her husband and has two grown children.

Stewart Emery is coauthor of the international bestsellers *Success Built to Last* and *Do You Matter?: How Great Design Will Make People Love Your Company*. He has a lifetime of experience as an entrepreneur, creative director, corporate culture consultant, and executive coach. He has led workshops and seminars and delivered keynotes all over the world.

Russ Hall is author of fourteen books and coauthor of numerous other books. He has also had short stories, essays, and articles published in a wide array of media and has received several awards.

Heather Ishikawa is the National Sales Director for Pearson TalentLens. Ishikawa has extensive experience in architecting corporatewide, assessment-based leadership development initiatives. Ishikawa has delivered workshops to hundreds of leaders on the topics of critical thinking, leadership, teambuilding, communication, and change management. She lives in California with her husband and two children.

John Maketa is the Director of Strategic Partnerships for Pearson TalentLens. Maketa is a dynamic leader in enterprise growth, developing bold and creative strategic alliances that catapult global performance and profit. Maketa is known throughout the learning and development industry as a major connector who is able to strategically align initiatives for parties on both sides of the table with unparalleled financial and professional success. He lives in Pennsylvania with his wife and son.

Introduction

Change your thinking... transform your life might seem like an extravagant benefit to claim for a book. However, if you do change the way you think to support the experiences and success that matter to you, your life *will* be transformed.

It is literally true that you feel the way you do because you think the way you do. To be in a loving and nurturing relationship requires patterns of thinking that create and make this quality of relationship possible. To experience satisfying professional success requires the ability to think in a way that will bring you this. Steve Jobs epitomizes that successful people think differently. Everything you want in your life demands the thinking styles that make it so. And, of course, anything you are experiencing that you don't want is because your thinking is not up to the task of bringing you what you do want. Instead, your way of thinking perpetuates your existing situation.

If you accept that this is, in fact, the case (and it is), the question becomes: Can you actually learn to think in a way to bring you the life you hunger for, or did you have to be born with a mind that was hardwired for highly effective thinking? Yes, you can learn to be a highly effective thinker. And no, research reveals that nobody is born hardwired to be able to do this. Highly effective thinkers are made and not born. This is a major discovery. We have learned that the wherewithal for you to live a wonderful life is an ability you develop in the process of living. You can do it, and yes, we can help.

We have also learned over the years of supporting people in the realization of their dreams that information is mostly overrated. With the advent of the Internet, there is no shortage of information. Any of us with an Internet-enabled device has universal access to information overload. We have seen very little improvement in the quality of the human experience as a result. Do you feel emotionally more connected in this brave new information age as a result of trying to consume more information? Deep inside, do you feel more confident that you can produce the results in the world and your life that really matter to you as you attempt to devour one more morsel of information? Is information feeding your soul? Although your mileage may vary, most of the people we ask reply, "Not so much."

So we have to conclude that there is little, if any, transformational power in the information. Transformation requires an experience that moves the human heart. Once upon a long time ago, certainly way, way back before the Internet began, or even the printed word, the kind of learning we are talking about here took place at the feet of the storyteller. With this in mind, we begin this book with a story of transformation that we hope will move your human heart.

In the story, you will meet a team of people who take it upon themselves to save the life of a little girl. Her name is Amenah, and at the beginning of the story, she is living and dying in a sheepherding village in Iraq. If the process of her dying is going to be transformed to become her experience of being truly alive, a great deal of first-class thinking must be done by an extended group of people from a village in Iraq to a hospital in Tennessee.

What do a war-torn town in Iraq, a bunch of Marines, an assortment of people back in the States, and a tiny sick girl have to do with critical thinking and the quality of your life? You might well ask.

When examples of good, successful thinking occur, they shine like gems and should be shared. That's what happens here. That's what the first part of this book is about. Here is a shining example set by people who seek to save the life of a terminally ill two-year-old Muslim girl in circumstances where wave upon wave of challenges, problems, and difficulties stretch their abilities to think their way through. This is a hero's journey—people just like you who become a team of heroes, actually. You will journey with them as they deploy highly effective thinking to transcend rational, emotional, and political challenges along the way.

At the outset, the team must deal with the military establishment's reluctance to get involved in a non-military intervention carrying considerable political risk if the mission ends in failure. They must then earn the trust of Muslim Tribal Elders who are opposed to a female Muslim infant travelling with male military personnel to the United States for life-saving treatment. On the journey they are confronted with the crisis of Amenah, who is critically ill, running out of oxygen at 30,000 feet. The medical extraction team must use their heads if they are to keep her alive.

By the time you are this far into the story you might be saying to yourself, "Self, quality thinking matters!"

After the story, it becomes all about you, and your thinking styles and your abilities. How do you keep alive the inspiration of what these people accomplished in your relationships, your work—your daily life? How do you think and act like these heroes? Well, you start with the recognition that heroes are ordinary people who do extraordinary things. You trace the patterns of effective thinking deployed by the people seeking a miracle for Amenah and learn how to use them for yourself. You complete an assessment to discover the strengths of your own thinking style. Next, you start using the set of simple tools and continuing support provided to develop these strengths and build the life of your dreams.

First then, here is the story. The names have not been changed. Please keep reading and then start doing, and then you will have the life you have always wanted!

Amenah's Story

The Humvee pulled up with a soft whoosh of tires on sandy gravel as near to the house as the driver could get. Marine Major Kevin Jarrard climbed out, tugged at his winter fatigues, and looked around, taking in the places where someone might hide—where they could take cover themselves if it came to that. By 2007, most of the insurgents had been driven out of this area, but there were incidents daily and it was wise to wear caution like an extra coat. This house, on the northern outskirts of Haditha, was no mansion, yet it was no appliance box either—a humble but functioning home for a shepherd with several children. The sky showed the rumpled gray of clouds bunching for a possible December rain, even snow. A breeze that swept across the Euphrates tugged at his short hair. He reached to tug his collar up higher against the chill. Born and raised in Georgia, he had never welcomed winter. But if you want warm sunny days and white picket fences, stay back in the United States.

He nodded to the surgeon, who climbed out of the vehicle with the interpreter. As they moved toward the house, Navy Captain John Nadeau asked a question with his eyes. Kevin's checking on Alaa Thabit Fatah, the father, hadn't confirmed that he'd been one of the insurgents, or that he hadn't been. He shrugged. That didn't seem to ruffle Nadeau, though only two years ago, the local police set up by the invading U.S. troops had been taken by insurgents to the town's soccer stadium and had been beheaded, left there to lay with orders that no one touch the bodies. Haditha was more secure now, but peace is fragile, and never so much so as here. Kevin could only hear the wind rasping against the house they approached and no sporadic gunfire in the distance, which would not have surprised him.

Kevin could see his breath as he knocked at the door. The father opened it and they entered a room that had no fireplace or heat. John Nadeau rubbed his hands together and glanced toward Kevin, who could smell something cooking slowly in the kitchen that Amenah's mother had left to be in this room. Garlic, rice, maybe a touch of lamb, or sheep—not much, probably, and for a large family. He'd timed their visit away from a meal hour, knowing the Iraqi custom of lavishing whatever food they had on any visitor first.

The mother waited across the room beside the little girl. He'd been surprised during his last visit when the mother had come out into the front room. Usually, the women stayed in a back room when other males visited. Now, Maha, the mother, gave the child a gentle nudge. Maha sat her down on the floor and Amenah looked at the visitors and started toward them with a flicker of mischievous eagerness in her eyes that quickly faded as the two-year-old stumbled, caught herself, struggled for her breath, and then kept coming. As she did, her complexion changed from its normal coloration to a dark blue that heightened in her lips and fingers.

John knelt, had his stethoscope out, warmed it with his hands, and started to examine the child, a customary practice in Iraq, where all examinations are done in front of the extended family. John had the bald pate with vestigial buzzed tonsure of silver hair of someone in his sixties. That and his confident manner evoked confidence among those who didn't know he was also a professor of medicine at Vanderbilt. Kevin liked to watch John work, whether at the sheik's home, or as they were now, in the home of a shepherd. He owed his life to John, as did many of his men. John wasn't really here to practice medicine on the civilians, but the mission of the Marines had shifted in the past couple of years, and troops were in the active role of trying to ease control over to the Iraqi police and Iraqi Army. So, when Sergeant Velasquez, Lima Company's squad leader, came across Amenah and her father, who had asked for help and said she would probably die without it, Kevin had made his first visit to the house and had seen enough to bring battlefield surgeon John along this time.

Source: Marines—Mark Lamelza

Figure 1 Captain John Nadeau with Amenah and her family

While John made his examination, Kevin eased closer to Maha with the interpreter. He reached to his wallet and took out a worn and frayed-at-the-corners photograph of Kelly and their four kids. He held it out to her. His youngest daughter, Rachel, was not far from Amenah's age. Maha nodded, smiled, and returned the picture. It was something Kevin often did. It told the people there he was just like them, a man with a family, one with a wish for a peaceful, prosperous life for his children, just like they desired.

John finally put away his things and stood. That was that for now. "Can you help our daughter?" her father asked. As a devout Christian and honorable man, Kevin looked him in his brown, pained eyes and said, "I'll do all I can." At that precise moment, he could have no idea of the enormity of all that loomed ahead.

Out in the Humvee, as they closed their doors, Kevin turned to John.

"It looks like cyanotic congenital heart disease," John said. "I'd say a Tetralogy of Fallot, but that's something I don't have the equipment to confirm, not here or even in the largest cities of Iraq."

"Is that common here?"

John nodded. "It sure is. They drink water out of the Euphrates that you wouldn't even wash in, let alone drink. They use insecticides and pesticides everywhere without any thought. God knows what these women are exposed to when they're pregnant. So birth defects are much more common."

Kevin asked him, "What might we do about this?"

Nadeau said, "Well, not much in Iraq."

"Is this girl going to live long?"

"No. She's going to get a chest infection and that's death for her."

"Is she fixable?"

"Probably. But not here in Iraq."

"How might we go about getting her fixed?"

"We'd have to send her off to America somehow, get someone there to do it." John looked out the window at the buildings going by, probably not seeing them, but already flipping through the Rolodex in his mind.

Back at his command post, which was a bombed-out school building in the downtown area, Kevin sat on his little makeshift cot, his head in his hands. He spent some time in prayer. This was something much, much bigger than him. He felt insufficient to the task. If this was something that the Lord purposed to bring about through him, he prayed that the Lord might give him the wisdom and discernment about how to proceed.

*   *   *

The next morning, John looked up from his mug of coffee, the steam providing some warmth against another chilly day. Kevin Jarrard was walking toward him, his face a tangle of determination and worry. Only thirty-five years old, Kevin was through and through a man of unflinching resolve once he'd decided upon something.

Before Kevin could speak, John said, "I take it you've decided to do this impossible thing." Now didn't this just seem like a scene out of *M*A*S*H* where Hawkeye Pierce and Trapper John set off on some wacky, well-intentioned mission.

9

Kevin laughed, and sat down. "So, how do we go about it? I know I'll have to clear it with Lieutenant Colonel Bellon. But there are a lot of other t's to cross and i's to dot."

"Well, there sure are," John chuckled. "I can do what I can with the folks back at Vanderbilt as far as the operation and the hospital goes, but there's a lot of money involved. I'm going to need to be pretty persuasive."

"Well, you've been with them long enough. They might come through." Kevin rubbed at his right temple. "Then there's the cost of getting them to and from the states. You know we can't use military aircraft to transport them."

"Right. And then there are the five tribes. You have to clear this with them. The idea of sending a child off to a foreign place is going to light a few fuses."

One aspect that led Nadeau to believe Bellon might let them go out on this particular limb was that when Bellon took over as commander of the battalion, he allowed and encouraged Nadeau to see that every Marine in the battalion was trained to be comfortable in dealing with the common causes of death on the battlefield: bleeding from an extremity wound, tension pneumothorax, and an obstructed airway. All this was something that had never been done before, and there's no doubt it had saved lives. Bellon's was the kind of leadership that gave opportunity to do such things.

John said, "In America, if you show up in the emergency room and you're Amenah, it doesn't matter what it costs; somebody's going to take care of you. But here, that couldn't be done. So—Marines being Marines—I guess I can't tell you that you can't do something, because you'll just go and get it done. So I'd better do all I can to help you."

Kevin rose and started to walk off. But he stopped and turned his head back. "We're doing the right thing, aren't we?" It was a rhetorical question, but John nodded.

"You know, a lot of what we have to deal with over here is about death. Why can't it be about life just for once?"

John grinned. "No reason at all."

Kevin walked away. Well, there were a lot of reasons, but possibly they were fixable, just like Amenah.

As soon as he got back to his computer, John fired off an e-mail to Dr. Karla Christian, a pediatric cardiac surgeon at Vanderbilt. He had known and worked with her for years and was confident she would help. She had the expertise to do open heart surgery. She had the facilities too, at the Monroe Carell Jr. Children's Hospital at Vanderbilt University in Nashville, Tennessee. If she said yes, this was still, by no means, a slam dunk. As Kevin had said, there were lots of "t's and i's" to go.

Source: Marines—Mark Lamelza

Figure 2 Major Kevin Clark, Major Mark Lamelza, Captain Krumenacker, Lieutenant Colonel David Bellon, Captain John Nadeau, Sergeant Major Wayne Rumore

11

*   *   *

Major Mark A. Lamelza, operations officer, sat behind his desk talking with the battalion's executive officer, Major Kevin Clark, who leaned against one side of the doorjamb. He suddenly straightened. Lieutenant Colonel David G. Bellon, the battalion commander, came barreling into the office.

Mark stood. David waved for him to sit back down as he lowered himself to the corner of the desk.

"You'll never guess what Kevin Jarrard and Captain Nadeau want to do," David said. "They want to send a two-year-old Muslim girl halfway around the world to Nashville for an operation she can't get here."

"What?" Mark said. "Are you kidding me?"

"Wish I was." David filled them in on all he knew so far and then asked, "What do you think?"

Mark shook his head. "There are just too many things that could go sideways. We'd have to check it with higher up."

Higher up meant their regimental commanding officer, Colonel H. Stacy Clardy III. And he would have to clear something like this upward through his chain of command.

"Do you know what he told me the first day he met me?" Mark said. "He said, 'If you mess up, I will fire you.'"

"He told me the same thing," David said. They laughed.

"Well, I don't think we should do this," Mark said.

"Let me tell you about my chat with Kevin Jarrard," David said. "You know how it is. As you're listening, you're processing—you

12

know, active listening. You're picking up on the critical vulnerabilities. Where could this thing go wrong? You know, I'm watching the guy talking to me, who I know very well, and I'm looking at him. Is he tired? Has he thought this out? What kind of game is he on right now? Is he on his 'A' game, or not? Because sometimes even your best guys have bad days. You start by listening to their words, but you are really taking inventory of them. Sometimes you're thinking, 'Okay, this guy needs some coaching and how can I apply my social energy to help him succeed today?' But it was pretty clear to me, almost immediately, that Kevin had thought this out. He and Nadeau had talked this over before he talked to me, and he was dropping little data points along as he talked. He mentioned he'd talked with Nadeau because he knows I admire and respect Nadeau. So, very quickly, my mental inventory was, 'Okay, this thing isn't half-baked. They have already done some pretty solid work here.'"

"It sounds like you want to do this crazy thing," Mark said. He knew that technically, as a Navy Captain, John Nadeau outranked both Kevin Jarrard and David Bellon. But John wouldn't push himself, though his word had quite a bit of weight to it, "currency" in Mark's military view.

"Well, I do want to do it. But you two talk it over. I'm going to step out of the room for a spell."

As soon as David was out of hearing, Mark and Kevin Clark began to talk. Mark had already given the hard push back. It was like David to drop a little bomb like that in their office and then leave. They talked it over, debated the fine points, and by the time David returned, they had shifted to problem solving. They laid out the risks, and he laid out what he wanted to do.

13

"The mother has to go too," David said. "The tribes won't let a little girl travel alone, and the father's still on a watch list. Too iffy. Can't leave the country."

"Oh, this just gets better."

"I know. It is what it is. What else?"

Mark said, "You know, they're going to need passports from Iraq and visas from Homeland Security," Mark said.

"Jake Falcone's your man for that," David said. Jake was the battalion communications officer, who David knew had a Washington, D.C., background and could facilitate clearance and passports, both from Iraq and Homeland Security, for Amenah and her mother to enter the United States—no easy feat, and one that would involve him traveling to meet the right people and move things along.

Mark said, "You know, whenever you ask something like this of me, I think that there is much more. I need to find the why, why, why—to get the big picture. And one of my very first concerns, sir, is about benefits versus risks. This is a very strategic decision with strategic implications if things fail."

A key part of the big picture included the impact doing this would have on locals. The Marine mission at this time was to help build the capacity of the Iraqi police and Iraqi Army so they could assume the role of security—this in a time when it was hard to even keep the markets open so people had a place to sell their tomatoes. "If something goes wrong with this plan, and it easily could, that could jeopardize quite a bit," Mark said.

"I know," David said. "This isn't just about Kevin, Dr. Nadeau, and this little girl. It's about 1,800 Americans and 65,000 Iraqis. If we get lost in this, or if it goes sideways, we could derail a pretty fragile peace. Also, are we going to suck up assets that we really need to apply someplace else?"

What would weigh a lot is how much currency Lieutenant Colonel Bellon and his officers had built up with their commanding officer.

"All I have to say is if this had come up or if we'd presented it when we first got here, given Colonel Clardy's opening remarks to us, I think it would have been almost impossible to sell this to him," Mark said.

"Yeah," David agreed. "He would have fired us."

Source: Marines—Mark Lamelza

Figure 3 Lieutenant Colonel Bellon and Colonel Clardy

*   *   *

15

Kelly Jarrard, back in Gainesville, Georgia, got an e-mail from her husband telling her about Amenah. Though she was kept busy raising four small children on her own, she called a family friend, Robin Smith, at the BB&T Bank in Gainesville, Georgia, and started an account to raise part of the money for transportation. The effort could only be a quiet grassroots one at first because any word getting back to Iraq might jeopardize Amenah even getting to leave.

On December 14, 2007, Kevin's aunt, Janet Jarrard, opened her e-mail and rocked back in her chair for a moment when she found a similar but more complex request. Kevin said he was taking up a collection among the Marines, and had the hospital at Vanderbilt lined up, but he needed her help with a whole lot more. All Janet had to do was help raise almost $30,000 for commercial travel costs for both the mother and daughter to leave from and return to Iraq, ensure the family had a place to stay, that an interpreter could be on hand, find a medical team to get the family to and from America, make sure culturally appropriate foods were on hand, find a female escort, part nurse and part chaperone, and, oh, by the way, do all this quickly please, chop, chop.

Anyone else might have torn at their hair and run screaming into the woods. But not Janet. Time might be of the essence, but she never flinched. His e-mail told her he had begun the necessary steps for documentation, paperwork, clearance, and permission from his superiors. Fund-raising to bring a Muslim child and her mother to the Christian south was going to be no easy feat. Recall Pastor Terry Jones from Gainesville, Florida, the controversial person who burned the Koran in March of 2011, causing riots in the Middle East that resulted in numerous deaths, including UN workers and their wives. His actions marked one extreme of the grassroots mood. There was a lot of confusion and some prejudice

16

about Muslims. Kevin's appeal to those stateside was that a little girl's life was at stake. In the face of those who might say, "You can't save them all," he said, "But we might be able to save one." Janet's first thought was, "Now, how in the heck are we going to do it?" He was asking her to be the point person in Nashville. Then, like her counterparts overseas, she shrugged off the impossibilities and started figuring out ways to make it all happen.

At the time, she was in the middle of redoing her kitchen, but she dropped that and started sending out a flurry of e-mails about an Iraqi child who was dying and they needed funds and logistical help getting her to Vanderbilt. A new kitchen is one thing, she figured, but this was a life-and-death matter. So she opened herself to the tasks, but she also realized she couldn't do it all. She, like everybody she spoke to, believed this situation was a calling, something God was going to make happen and she was to be one small part of it. As she explained to a friend, "There is a power greater than us that is activated when we open ourselves up for it, uncap our individual wells of creativity, thinking, determination, obstinance, whatever you want to call it. Just opening oneself up to letting that information flow makes the difference."

And flow it did. Two enormously important things happened as a result of her e-mails. At that time, she was working for Tennessee Donor Services, doing public education and PR for the organ procurement organization for the state of Tennessee. One of the organ recovery coordinators who heard about Amenah's situation was Jonathan Malloch, who said, "How can I help?" He had a medical background, had EMT experience, and had worked with FEMA during the response to Hurricane Katrina. More important, he had an extensive military background with all the connections that went with that—he was exactly what Janet needed, someone who could speak the military as well as civilian language.

17

Even though he wouldn't be free to go along himself, he knew how the military worked, could assemble an extraction team of capable medics, could arrange for their diplomatic clearance, and he even said he'd see to the logistics of getting the mother and daughter out of Iraq into Jordan for their commercial flights. The second extraordinary event that happened as a result of Janet's reaching out was hearing from Deanna Dolan of World Relief, a nonprofit organization.

Deanna spoke some Arabic and was willing to help provide a full-time interpreter, Zainab, a woman whose life had been threatened in Iraq because she had translated for the U.S. troops. Deanna was also a member of the Grace Chapel Church in Lieper's Fork, Tennessee, just outside Nashville, where Steve Berger was the pastor. The church at once started a collection to help bring Amenah to America for the operation, and Steve and his wife Sarah even agreed to let mother and daughter, as well as Deanna and Zainab stay at their home to help provide orientation and help with planning culturally appropriate food.

Well, that was falling into place nicely, Janet thought. Because a female traveling chaperone was necessary, she also lined up her nurse friend, Lisa Van Wye, from Bowling Green, Kentucky, to make the trip to Jordan along with the extraction medical team to escort mother and daughter to America.

With funds slowly trickling in because they couldn't make a public call for funds until Amenah was safely out of Iraq, Janet had to go ahead and pay for the commercial flight tickets with her own credit card, trusting that the $7,000 she was laying out could be returned, and it soon was. Other than organizational meetings with Jonathan and the PR people at Vanderbilt, most of her frantic involvement was over by December, so she could take a deep breath and begin to relax. Somehow, getting that kitchen redone didn't seem quite so pressing at the moment.

*   *   *

"Good news," Jonathan Malloch said. He sat across the conference room table from Glenn Susskind and Gary White, two colleagues of his on the Disaster Medical Assistance team who had agreed to fly to Jordan to act as the extraction team. Outside, flecks of snow swirled down from a pensive sky over Chattanooga, although the drive to the D-MAT building that morning had been through fairly clear streets.

Glenn arched an eyebrow and Gary fiddled with his pen and pad.

"You saw my e-mail to Kevin Jarrard that we weren't going to be able to help like we'd hoped—that it was a 'no go' for us. Right?"

"Yeah, and we saw his reply to keep trying," Gary said.

"He sure does seem a man on a mission," Glenn agreed.

Jonathan nodded. "Kevin says arrangements are already in place at Vanderbilt. You've seen how he's keeping us up on everything over there. I take it that their regimental commander, a full bird colonel named Clardy, was visiting so Lieutenant Colonel Bellon arranged for Kevin to ask him for a helicopter to get to the Jordanian border. Clardy told Kevin that if everything comes together, the regiment would give him a helicopter. Now it's up to us to make sure everything in our piece is ready. That brings me to the best news yet. Blackwater Worldwide has agreed to help with the extraction, on their dime. This is huge. They'll escort you to the Jordanian border and back to Amman. They just want to vet you, and that's okay. You'll both stand up to that. You may even get briefed about everything, and I mean everything, even how to comb your hair."

"No problem," Glenn said. "I'm glad it's back on. I was really hoping to help see this through." He looked toward Gary.

"That's great," Gary agreed. "But I'll let Glenn go first. You know how I am when I get talking."

"Well, I've been going over all we need to pack, how much we can carry," Glenn said. He was the medic of the team, who'd also been with FEMA at Katrina and had recently gotten back from Haiti. His background included work in Arizona doing a lot of fixed-wing transports of moving patients over quite long distances. "I'm still running down what we can get in Jordan, and what we can bring or take out. Oxygen is going to be an issue."

"I looked into the cost for chartering a Galaxy 6," Gary said. "Way out of reach. An air medical agency is a quarter of a million for just one way. Scratch that. We'll have to figure out how to do this as best we can on a limited budget."

"We've both gone through the briefing material on Muslim-American relations, any cultural issues, the tribe this mother and daughter are from, so we should be okay there too," Glenn said.

"I appreciate you guys going, because I can't go, and Kevin Jarrard is still in theater over in Iraq, and Vanderbilt has no means of getting them here. The safety of you two is my top concern, which is why I'm glad we were able to get Blackwater involved. It looks like we're going to have to go with Royal Jordanian Airlines, though. It's all we can afford considering what's been gathered so far, and their chief medical officer has to approve the girl for travel or she's not getting on their planes," Jonathan said.

"Then we'll need a Plan B if we have to go by ground transportation," Gary said.

"And a Plan C if she gets worse, or dies," Glenn said.

*   *   *

Jake Falcone handed Kevin Jarrard the small pile of passports and visas. "This should be everything you need," he said. I don't mind telling you that I had to grease the occasional palm here and there on this side, and getting the stuff from Washington, D.C., well, it's D.C. after all. That was six weeks."

Kevin grinned. He knew how the State Department and Department of Homeland Security worked. "Thanks for all your travel and help on this." He was leafing through the documents as he spoke. "Oh, my gosh."

"What?"

"This passport is for Fatima. That's Amenah's seven-year-old sister!"

"Well, that's the information you gave me."

"I know. It's not you, Jake. I don't speak or write Arabic. What am I going to do? Their flight's in 72 hours!"

"I wish I could help, but I can't get away. If you can take them over to Baghdad, they could straighten it out in time over there."

"I've got a river clearing operation on the Euphrates. I can't do it."

"Well, call a cab then."

That's what Kevin did. First he called some of his Iraqi friends who had friends in the Department of the Interior in Baghdad. He would have to make one last gamble. He had less than 48 hours to get them to Baghdad, get an Iraqi passport, get them back to Haditha, and get them on a helicopter. He was not panicked, but he did not see how it would be possible. He raced to their house after midnight, woke up the mom and dad and Amenah, and said, "Look, I've got to get you to Baghdad tomorrow, we've only got one shot to make this happen."

Still before daylight in the morning, he loaded mother, father, and Amenah into a cab, paid the driver, and sent them hurtling off toward Baghdad.

Whew. Well, he'd done all he could.

After that chaotic start to what turned out to be another chaotic day, Kevin came back to his command post very late in the day. He was listening to reports and talking to some of his leaders when he got a frantic call from one of his checkpoints, "Sir, it's Captain Semir"—one of Kevin's Iraqi friends—"he's got to see you now, there's been a terrible emergency."

Kevin ran over to the checkpoint. Captain Semir said, "Sir, Amenah and her family have been shot up, there's been a terrible misunderstanding out on the highway."

The friendly fire incident happened five or six kilometers from town, so he scrambled vehicles and they raced on out. The sun had gone down. It was dark. They were on the highway heading out, and in the headlights of the Humvee Kevin was traveling in, he saw the taxi that he sent them out to Baghdad in that morning. They had been in that taxi at his orders. He was responsible for their lives. He saw bullet holes in the front windshield.

He was going to have to arrest some Iraqi soldiers. Everyone was shouting, waving arms, and rushing around. His vehicle stopped. He ran to the car, thinking, "I have killed an Iraqi mother, father, and daughter."

He ran to the side of the taxi, and there in the ditch is Alaa Thabit, the father, and Maha, the mother, with Amenah in her arms, rocking back and forth. They were okay.

The Iraqi army had received a report about some bad guys in a vehicle of similar description, and had shot the vehicle thinking it was the bad guys. Miraculously, no one was harmed. The bullets had passed through the top of the car and missed them, and nobody was harmed. And...they had the passport. They had managed to get Amenah's passport. Kevin was on his knees in the dirt with his eyes closed, thinking, "Thank you, thank you, thank you, Lord, for preserving the lives of my friends."

*   *   *

With 12 hours to go before getting them onto a helicopter, Kevin got called to a tribal "powwow" with all of the mother's brothers, all of the male members of her family. He took his interpreter and a couple of Iraqi friends, but soon found himself sitting across the room from them; they were armed and didn't look happy.

He knew when he walked into the room that this wasn't good. He could sense that there was some tension here, and couldn't figure out why until they started talking. They said, "Listen, we've decided that we're not going to allow our sister Maha to travel to America without a male member of her family. That would be dishonoring to our family."

Kevin said, "So, wait a minute, you would prefer to see your niece die than allow your family to be dishonored?"

They said, "Yes, exactly."

Kevin told his interpreter to tell them some things, and the interpreter said, "Sir, I don't think that's a good idea." So, he had a

23

moment to reconsider. It was a good thing, he thought later, that he didn't speak good Arabic or it might have just turned into a shooting match. They looked ready for it. Their hands rested ready by their weapons.

What he told them was, "Listen. You know me and I know you. And I'm going to give you my word of honor that your sister will not be in the presence of an American male without a female escort. I will ensure that she has a female escort wherever she goes, and that's the best I can do. I'm giving you my word. I'm just simply asking that you trust me."

They chattered among themselves, often with the heated waving of arms. Eventually, Sheik Said Flayah Othman from the al-Jughayfi tribe, who spoke for all of them, said, "Your word is enough."

Source: Marines—Mark Lamelza

Figure 4 Major Kevin Jarrard, Sheik Said Flayah Othman, tribal chief from the al-Jughayfi tribe, Lieutenant Colonel Bellon

*   *   *

Before morning, Kevin had arranged to have one of the female Iraqi interpreters travel with them to the border checkpoint. She was along when Kevin picked up Amenah and her mother, who had never been out of Haditha, Iraq, in her life. As the CH-53 helicopter they would travel in landed, Kevin watched the mother's eyes get big. She must have thought this was like something from outer space.

Source: Marines—Mark Lamelza

Figure 5 Major Kevin Jarrard holds Amenah before she leaves Haditha, Iraq.

Their destination, hours away, was where Highway 10 crosses the Iraqi-Jordan border at Trebil. As they flew west, a blinding snowstorm developed. It doesn't snow in western Iraq very often. If that helicopter had been 10 or 15 minutes late getting into Haditha, they wouldn't have made it to Trebil before the whiteout hit.

The snow was thick and all around them and they had only a 10- or 15-minute window to get the helicopter onto the ground, get Amenah and her mother to the checkpoint at the border, and into the arms of the American team there. A few handshakes and hugs, some prayers, and off they went, disappearing into the snow. At that point, all Kevin could do was pray that all would be well. He had time for that. He was snowed in and couldn't go back to Haditha himself for two days.

*   *   *

Gary White sat in the lead vehicle and waited. They all looked out the windows and watched. Glenn Susskind was in the medical vehicle parked behind theirs. The third vehicle, parked behind that, one the Blackwater men referred to as a "bump" vehicle, was along just in case anything happened to one of the other two.

He looked up at the dark clouds and was glad he wasn't the one in a four-hour helicopter ride. Snow swirled around them and covered the ground and had begun to drift.

"I thought it never snowed here," he said.

"It doesn't," the interpreter said. "Not like this, anyway. I haven't seen anything like this in years." She was another part of the puzzle Blackwater had already helped fix when the original interpreter they'd arranged for didn't work out. The Blackwater guys had also helped Glenn get all the extra medical supplies he needed too— oxygen, food, water, even IV fluids.

Now they waited, and watched it snow.

The 280 miles from Amman to the Jordanian border had taken three-and-a-half hours after leaving at 4:30 a.m. When they'd come to each of the many checkpoints, vehicles had queued up in long lines, but those checking the vehicles had moved the barriers and waved the Blackwater caravan through each time. Going back was going to be a whole different can of beans with all this snow.

Then began a scene like out of a TV show. First they saw the lights, and then the shapes of two helicopters emerged from the blur of falling snow. One of the helicopters eased to the ground. The other continued to circle above, keeping a tight and secure perimeter. It waited for the helicopter on the ground to empty.

Gary and Glenn got out of their vehicles and went to the check-point with the Blackwater team and the interpreter to greet the mother and daughter. As they moved through the snow, Kevin Jarrard was grinning like it was Christmas. They could see relief on his face too, and the hugs all around were firm and genuine. The other helicopter spun and took off. Kevin sure smiled a lot for someone who was going to be stuck on the ground there for a while.

Glenn and the female Navy corpsman, a medic from Kevin's team, were both taking a quick look at Amenah and assessing her, exchanging information, and the interpreter was helping with the Arabic. Amenah was blue. She had a runny nose and all the typical signs of an upper respiratory infection. She had a fever. Through the interpreter, they learned that this was not how she usually was. So they'd been brought a child who was sick on top of being sick. They were well dressed for the cold and snow but Amenah was very dehydrated. They checked her blood pressure and pulse and oxygen saturation. Her sats (saturations) were low, lower than they apparently had been day to day. The stress and whatever

27

infection she had going on was getting to her. It was time they started back to Amman.

"Oh, and one other thing," the Navy medic said, "The mother is diabetic. Here's her insulin."

"Great," Glenn said. He'd been hoping to meet a physician and get an extensive report. But it was what it was. Gary was already starting to watch how she moved, considering whether she was going to have trouble handling the plane rides or walking through airports.

Kevin and his group had turned and now scurried back to their helicopter, which had shut down its prop, a sign they were probably not going to try to fly back to Haditha that day.

Glenn, Gary, Amenah, her mother, the interpreter, and Lisa Van Wye, Janet Jarrard's nurse friend who Kevin had promised would be a female chaperone, all loaded into the medical vehicle, and when everyone was inside, the small caravan turned and started back toward Amman in what was already half a foot of snow with more coming down.

In addition to snacks, fresh fruit, Gatorade, and other supplies for the road, Glenn had also brought along a small DVD player, along with a couple of Disney DVDs like Mickey Mouse. That entertained Amenah enough for Glenn to assess her as they rolled along.

Still, the journey back was long. Perhaps it felt more so because Amenah was tired, agitated, and cranky, as any child that age with a fever and a runny nose would be, on top of travel fatigue and not being able to catch her breath. Put a child like that in a crowded Suburban, her mother at constant arm's reach, for almost four hours and it's nobody's idea of a jolly time.

They breathed a collective large sigh when they pulled up at the five-star InterContinental Hotel, one of the finest in Amman, where Blackwater had made arrangements. The staff had been carefully preprepared for their arrival. They put them in rooms in the center of a hallway. There were no other guests in that whole hallway. They had cleared the hallway at Blackwater's request. It was quite secure. Amenah and her mother were in one room, and Glenn and Gary had the adjoining rooms. Once settled, they could do a better assessment on Amenah, and start working on getting the fever down, getting her hydrated, and giving her some cough medicine. They did everything they could to prepare her for travel, while trying to be the least invasive as possible. They had strong concerns because now she had a cold and was even that much sicker.

Glenn made a call to the Vanderbilt hospital and spoke with Dr. Thomas Doyle, a pediatric cardiologist who would be working with Dr. Karla Christian. Glenn told him, "Hey, this is not the picture that we've had painted. When we get back, you need to be ready for a really sick kid, not a semihealthy one."

From their assessment at the hotel, they knew that Amenah was going to require oxygen, especially once the plane gained enough altitude to pressurize. There was no way they could carry enough oxygen for a 14-hour flight. The flight would be stressful for all, but especially for the two-year-old.

When Lisa Van Wye, Gary White, Glenn Susskind, Amenah, her mother, and their Blackwater escort got to the airport, they were told at the ticket counter that Amenah needed to see the airline's doctor to get her health certified. They were escorted quite a distance, through what looked to Glenn like the bowels of the airport, to where a doctor examined Amenah, said she was okay to fly, and he gave them authorization to take oxygen onto the plane. Then they passed through multiple security stations and found that on the plane, a male flight attendant on the Royal Jordanian Airlines is the lead person on each flight. He also makes a determination of whether or not anybody can get on the flight, and he reports to the pilot, who gets to make a determination again about if anybody can get on the flight.

Once they had those hurdles behind them, they tried to upgrade Amenah to get her in First Class, but that didn't work out. They all sat in the Coach section, though they got a whole row, all the way in the back. Most of the stewardesses, including the steward, didn't speak English at all, except one who had family in the states and was very fluent. Because they were without an interpreter, her presence was very helpful. Another passenger, who was Jordanian but was an American psychiatrist, a doctor, helped them with the translation issues too.

They had the oxygen generators, but knew they needed one to get them from Chicago to Nashville. They hoped that about 8 hours of oxygen in the generators would be enough for a 14-hour flight. They hoped that they would be able to wean her a little bit at take-off and landing, so she wouldn't need as much oxygen. That did not work out to be the case.

They watched her pulse oximeter the whole way, and her oxygen would get very low, low to the point where she would actually start getting a little bit sluggish and a little bit air hungry. So they opted to leave her on a higher concentration of oxygen through the beginning of the flight, hoping they would get her to fall asleep and decrease her oxygen needs. That also didn't work out.

Seven hours into the flight, Glenn and Gary realized they would not have enough oxygen, so their backup plan became to utilize some of the airplane's oxygen. The steward wasn't happy about that, but they were able to convince him that they didn't need to use all of the plane's oxygen. They could probably get by with one or two tanks. So they used what would be the emergency oxygen for passengers. They had to manipulate the tanks somewhat. The plane's administration system was completely different from anything they had seen before. Glenn managed to rig up something that would get her oxygen the whole way home, and they literally finished their last liter of oxygen as they were landing in Chicago.

They didn't really have a contingency to go to a Chicago hospital, but they had a contingency in case she got very ill and they had to fly her on an air ambulance from Chicago to Nashville. They checked her again, and though she was cranky, tired, and feverish, they deemed her strong enough for one more flight. They headed for the airplane where they had a battery-operated oxygen generator waiting for the Chicago to Nashville part of the trip.

*   *   *

Deanna Dolan, with World Relief, their Arabic interpreter Zainab, Pastor Steve Berger of Grace Chapel Church in Lieper's Fork, Tennessee, along with Kelly Jarrard, Kevin's wife, and her four children were there at the Nashville airport to greet Amenah, her mother, Lisa, Gary, Glenn, and their Blackwater escort. Several news crews from varied media were on hand too, now that it was safe to talk about the effort to save Amenah. When Amenah's mother saw Kelly, she went to the mother and four kids and gave each a warm hug and kiss. She said it was from Major Jarrard back in Iraq, who had showed her pictures and said he missed them very much.

31

The news stations wanted footage and their stories, but Deanna thought Amenah did not look well at all, so the welcoming group sought to keep everything low key. Amenah's lips were blue, her face blue. She looked like she needed oxygen. Still, she tottered across and into the pastor's arms. Maha looked exhausted and overwhelmed, but pleased that so many people wanted to be supportive.

With a few last words of care from the extraction team, Deanna, Steve, and Zainab took the mother and daughter to the Bergers' home, which sits on five acres, with a river that winds through the back of the property, surrounded by the 43 acres of the church grounds and then several farms of over 200 acres, all very secluded and private.

That evening, Amenah seemed to be getting so little oxygen in her bloodstream that it was amazing she was functioning at all. Deanna and the Bergers wondered how she could even be conscious. And she did pass out a couple of times that night. The mother would just splash water on her face. For the mother, that was kind of normal. That's all she'd known for that child since she was born. So the mother wasn't freaking out, but Steve and Sarah had to hold their emotions in check. They were scared, afraid that the little girl was going to die.

*   *   *

On January 24, 2008, at 11:00 a.m., Amenah arrived at the Monroe Carell Jr. Children's Hospital at Vanderbilt for a chest X-ray and initial exam to diagnose her heart problem. She was very tired and cranky. Deanna knew Amenah had only gotten about three hours of sleep. Maha seemed tired too, but serene. Her daughter was finally going to get the kind of help she so desperately needed. Maha greeted all the new strangers with warmth. Her interpreter, though, told Deanna that Maha was afraid. She worried about Amenah and what could happen at the hospital. All along the way, mother and child were reassured through their interpreter that she would not experience anything painful today—they just wanted some special pictures to see what was wrong with Amenah's heart.

In the Pediatric Cardiology Clinic, Dr. Karla Christian, after finding more complications and additional infections, especially did not like what she saw from the child's first-ever chest X-ray. Her colleague, Dr. Thomas Doyle, and the staff performed an echocardiogram. After the tests, Doyle called a medical interpreter together with the interpreter who had been working with the family and explained to Amenah's mother what they'd found. Amenah's heart was not only backward, but, in addition, the blood flow to her lungs was restricted and her major arteries were out of place. Because of the stress of travel, a fever she was running, and an oxygen level that was very low, they placed her in an intensive care unit. Steve and Sarah Berger, the host family, and Deanna Dolan made sure that Amenah and her mother got some culturally appropriate food and walked them to settle into their room in the main hospital.

Dr. Christian told the mother and those who had come with Amenah, "She will require a complex open heart surgery with significant risk." They first had to get the child healthy enough for an operation. An aspect of the procedure they planned also took into consideration what kind of medical care the girl would get when she returned home. They would have to do everything they could to make sure she was as self-sustaining as possible.

In the week before her operation, Amenah lost her blue tinge and began to show a deep dimple in her right cheek that appeared when she giggled. She waved vigorously at visitors and said, "Bye," or "Habebi," which means sweetheart in Arabic. Her parted hair was in pigtails and she clutched her stuffed toy. She was in America. She was safe.

Amenah and her mother even got a preoperation visit by the Iraqi ambassador to the United States, Samir Sumaidaie, on Sunday, January 27. The ambassador is also from Haditha. He said that efforts like this are important, especially in times of war. "War is a cruel thing. Many families get destroyed or disrupted, but there are instances where lives are saved—many instances," Sumaidaie said. He expressed his "appreciation to the American military that never miss a chance when it is possible to save lives."

On February 11, Amenah was well enough for the operation. The Berger family arrived at 5:30 a.m. at the Children's Hospital with their guests, Amenah and her mother. Amenah's mother was very quiet, obviously feeling very anxious about the surgery, but Amenah, blissfully unaware at age two, hopped onto a trike and played until she was called back to a holding room to prepare for surgery.

By 7:00 a.m., surgeon Karla Christian, M.D., anesthesiologist Brian Donahue, M.D., and several other staff members had stopped in to explain the procedure to Amenah's mother, through the interpreter Zainab. Amenah's mother was also told what she could expect to see when she was allowed to visit Amenah in the recovery area in the Children's Hospital's Pediatric Critical Care Unit. She was told Amenah would still be asleep, would be on a ventilator, and would have several tubes and wires attached to various parts of her body, as is typical for any child undergoing open heart surgery.

Maha confided in Deanna, "Is she going to make it out alive from the surgery?" Several women from the church had come to support Maha and Amenah, and Maha asked them if they would pray. They did. She relaxed and they kidded around, keeping Maha's mind distracted.

As Dr. Doyle had put it, "Untreated, this will be a fatal condition in her young childhood." They had to operate, and they did. Dr. Christian performed the operation, and, in effect, they had to reroute blood to her lungs. For the rest of her life, she will have only one pumping chamber instead of two. The logic was that she would be back in Iraq, where she could not get repeat attention. Doyle said, "It's going to sustain her for the rest of her life in a village where she has little medical care or very little access to any medical personnel. That's her only option."

The operation was a success, and Amenah was put on a ventilator for several hours. After a critical 24 hours had passed after the surgery, the doctors announced they were optimistic Amenah would have a full recovery. Amenah was next taken to the Pediatric Critical Care Unit and soon weaned from the ventilator. By Wednesday morning, she was back to blowing kisses and waving at the nurses and staff who dropped by to check up on her.

It was not long before Amenah was well enough to return to the Bergers' home where they had become one big family. Maha had her normal enough ups and downs, missing her culture and her family. They bought her all the food she needed to cook Iraqi meals. She would sit on the kitchen floor at Steve and Sarah's house and cook, and teach Sarah how to cook. She even made her own yoghurt, which she stored in the refrigerator. Deanna said, "She wanted to go shopping a lot. And we would take her shopping.

35

In fact, when she went back, I don't think she could fit everything in her suitcase that she got."

A little more than two weeks after her surgery, Amenah came back for a final checkup at the Children's Hospital. Amenah had another echocardiogram, to make sure the blood flow in her heart was still running through the right pipes at the right rate—it was. Then Christian checked out the sound of her heart, checked out her scar for any signs of infections or problems, and found none.

Source: World Relief—Deanna Dolan

Figure 6   Deanna Dolan and Amenah

Little Amenah, Deanna noticed, turned out to be a ham, enjoying all the attention she was getting from the family, those at church, and the media. It tickled Deanna to see Amenah's change from being a fussy, lethargic little girl into one full of life, who was sunny and making jokes. She had a pair of tiny sneakers that would squeak every time she walked. At church, Pastor Steve would be preaching and everyone would hear a "squeak, squeak, squeak" and the whole church would crack up. They'd fallen in love with the little girl from across the world.

Source: World Relief—Deanna Dolan

Figure 7   Amenah getting around quite well after her operation

The day when Amenah and Maha were to get on a plane with Kevin Jarrard's wife Kelly to make the flight back to Jordan, Deanna said, "It was very emotional. Everybody was crying, even Steve and Sarah's children were crying. Maha was crying. Maha grabbed Steve's neck and wouldn't let go. Now that's unusual because her being a Muslim woman, she would normally not interact with a man that way. She really loved Pastor Steve."

Then the plane lifted into the air over Nashville and flew away, taking quite a few hearts tugging along with it.

*　　*　　*

On March 11, 2008, President George W. Bush landed in *Air Force One* at the Nashville airport and met Dr. Karla Christian. He had these words to say to the press about her. "This is Dr. Christian, Dr. Karla Christian, who really symbolizes the best of America. She and a team of hers have performed surgery on a little Iraqi girl who was discovered by United States Marines. People in Nashville raised the money for the family; they were supported by the Marines there in Iraq; some of the Marines raised money; and they sent this little girl, whose heart was ailing, to America, right here to Nashville. And Karla and her team healed the little girl and she's back in Iraq. And the contrast couldn't be more vivid. We got people in Iraq who murder the innocent to achieve their political objectives—and we've got Americans, who heal the broken hearts of little Iraqi girls. Ours is a compassionate nation that believes in the universality of freedom—and ours is a nation full of loving souls that when they find a stranger in need will lend their God-given talents to help that stranger. And that's precisely what happened."

*　　*　　*

Kelly Jarrard and Glenn Susskind flew with Amenah and her mother from Nashville back to Amman, Jordan. Then, for the last leg of the journey, from Amman to Baghdad, Kevin didn't have a female able to accompany the mother and daughter. So, with the surgery successful and her coming home, he had to head back to the family for another powwow with the brothers, one he didn't welcome, because the last one had nearly led to gunfire.

He told them, "Listen. I have kept my word to you. I promised you that your sister Maha would not be dishonored. And I have her and Amenah in Amman, Jordan. But I do not have anyone who can fly with them from Amman to Baghdad. So you've got two options. They can stay in Amman, and I don't have any way to care for them, or you can permit her to fly the last leg on a Royal Jordanian Airlines unescorted. We'll fly her home from Baghdad."

There was a hesitant moment, then they finally said, "Go ahead, proceed."

Kevin knew he had done his very best to keep his word.

On March 7, Kevin picked up Amenah's father, Alaa Thabit, and they grabbed a CH-53 helicopter down to the Marine base in western Iraq, Al Asad. There they got onto a Marine aircraft, a C-130 to Baghdad, and landed in Baghdad. They were on the C-130, looking out the windows and saw the Royal Jordanian Airline plane land. Soon, a Blackwater truck came across the tarmac and Kevin and Alaa Thabit stepped out to greet a healthy, pretty, and far happier Amenah who shot across to dive into her father's embrace. Kevin and Maha joined in what became a tearfully joyful group hug that went on until Kevin told Amenah, "Let's get you home."

In the late afternoon, with the sun setting over the Euphrates River Valley, the MV-22 Osprey that took them the final leg back to Haditha landed on a soccer field, once the center of civic life in the area and now a landing zone. A cheering crowd of Iraqis awaited them.

Source: Marines—Mark Lamelza

Figure 8 Amenah and her mother on the way to Baghdad when heading home

Source: Marines—Mark Lamelza
Photo by Sergeant Shawn Coolman

Figure 9 Amenah reunited with her father at Baghdad

Kevin was thinking again about how only two years before, the insurgents in Iraq had rounded up the officers of the police force the U.S. troops had supported and brought them to this same stadium and had them beheaded, then gave the order that anyone who touched the bodies would be subject to the death penalty. So, when a helicopter landed to a cheering crowd of Iraqis and little Amenah was carried off, clutching a pink bunny and being touched by her siblings, and the stadium was filled once again with joy, Kevin felt it was the perfect juxtaposition between the al Qaeda and America. Al Qaeda comes bringing death, tyranny, and terror, whereas the United States comes bringing life and liberty.

He let Amenah and Maha and Alaa Thabit go on their own back to the vehicle, and he spent a moment just soaking in the scene. Back at the family's little home just north of town, where Amenah's story had started for him, some of the Iraqi businessmen in town had put together a huge feast with tents and celebrations and all the rest, and they all spent the rest of that night really soaking in all that had transpired.

Could he have done it alone? No, he admits. "Every one of those decisions that was made was the result of the totality of my experiences throughout everything that had happened to me up to that point in my life," he said. "There were many people without whose efforts at any given point this operation would have fallen apart. So, certainly the situation was much bigger than me. I was privileged to play some small part and be glad for that." As Kevin Jarrard put it to all of them, "Words are inadequate to describe my thankfulness to all of you for your roles in this mission. If you have never previously witnessed a miracle—now you have. Semper Fidelis and God Bless."

What Is a Miracle?

When we think of a miracle, in a medical context such as this, we often think in terms of something like a magic wand or divine intervention—one minute you are very, very sick and the next moment, POOF, you are better. A miracle is also sometimes thought of as a perceptible interruption of the laws of nature. That is more the case here. A little girl would have died, but she didn't.

A miracle can be a fortuitous event, which includes finding Amenah in time, assembling the means and people to move a Muslim child from a war zone almost halfway around the world to stay in a Christian southern setting, fixing her, and bringing her back to Haditha, Iraq, ready to live a healthy life.

This epitomizes a miracle as any statistically unlikely but beneficial event, such as surviving a terminal illness and "beating the odds" while doing so. Just think of all the factors involved: local Iraqi prejudice against allowing women or children to be alone with strangers, the difficulties of transporting a terminally sick child out of a war zone and such a long distance, the risk if she died in transport or during the operation, the need to raise money for travel because the military couldn't foot that bill, the need for an interpreter to bridge the language gap, a place to stay in America, people to escort the child and mother to and from Iraq to commercial flights out of Jordan, and many more bumps and curves in the road.

But the real miracle here is the orchestration of people and resources all to save the life of one little girl from a country where thousands had died. Moreover, all of the people involved on both sides of the ocean in making this happen were different, thought differently, and went about their lives based on varied thinking styles and approaches. That's what we are about to explore in greater depth—the kind of thinking that you can use in your own life. You will find that when you change your thinking, you can change your career...and that's a miracle worth desiring and looking into, as you will here.

How Your Mind Works—Some Assembly Required

Thinking is something we all do, so you might have assumed others just do it better than you, or at least differently. Well, you might be partially right—for the moment. But here's the really huge thing. You *can* get better at it. Thinking is a skill, not an inherent gift, so it's something you can improve upon. That's right. You can get really quite good at it. People who you admire—like those in "Amenah's Story," who step up and take action based on taking careful and considered steps, who can weigh risk, and who live fuller, richer lives as a consequence—represent the kind of person you can become.

Take, for example, the medical people. When Captain John Nadeau, Dr. Karla Christian, or Dr. Thomas Doyle leap to action, they do so by studying everything they can learn about a patient or a situation. They proceed with haste when they must, but with caution when they can. Yet each has a different background, home life, and, for that matter, way they go about thinking. John is a hypertension specialist for adults, whereas Karla is a pediatric cardiac surgeon, and Thomas is a pediatric cardiologist. In Nashville, Karla and Thomas faced surprising challenges in fixing Amenah, but they were working within the groove of their specialties, the core of their practiced expertise. John, on the other hand, is used

45

to having to make do in quite diversified settings—one minute attending to the needs of adults in a combat setting and in the next minute, figuring out what is wrong with a little girl and what to do about it. He has the kind of mind that says, "Hey, if every Marine had some of the life-saving techniques of a medic, more lives of American Marines could be saved. How do we go about making that happen?"

Consider also that the contexts of the problems needing resolution were quite different. John had to decide: What's wrong with this child? Can it be fixed here? Where can it be fixed? How do we go about that? Karla and Thomas, at Vanderbilt's Children's Hospital, had a different situation: How do we repair this girl's heart and body so she can live the best life possible in a place where ongoing or future medical help won't be available?

Whether you think life in the medical field is outside your grasp, or even if that's exactly where you are headed, you will need to hone your thinking skills to be, as John is, ready for anything. If you are like Glenn Susskind and Gary White, the medics in the extraction team who escorted Amenah to America, you are going to have to face situations where multiple scenarios are possible, and you have to be prepared for each. Or you might even be like Janet Jarrard, Major Kevin Jarrard's aunt who was peacefully minding her own business in Tennessee when she was suddenly called upon to make numerous and complex preparations in a very short time frame. You might even be in a managerial role and ask yourself, as Lieutenant Colonel David Bellon did, "How can I work within a system that has a rigid hierarchy and established protocols and give those who report to me the opportunities to sparkle at what they do by testing the barriers of what can be done and what should be done?"

The thing you can take away from all the stories of the varied participants in "Amenah's Story" is that they all put their minds to work, and their quite different ways of going about that thinking and doing is what wove the tapestry that made a miracle happen. No one of them could have done this alone, and they all had to work in their unique ways and to their own strengths. These were people like you performing extraordinary feats by working together, using their minds to achieve a greater good.

You think all the time, and whether you know it or not, you have a distinct thinking style, a way of going about what you do. If you've ever thought you'd like to better understand how that works or, more important, improve upon your thinking abilities in a way that can transform your life, you are taking the right step seeking to explore your possibilities for becoming the best thinker you can be.

To understand how, let's take a look at three important areas of your mind: dreams, feelings, and thinking. This trinity of the mind is like a three-person rowing team. You have dreams calling out direction while thinking and feeling do the rowing. When all three are in sync, you glide through life. Of course, they are not always in perfect synchrony, so let's look more carefully at the role each plays.

Dreams

The hospital's walls leaned or had fallen into the structurally risky shambles of a building in the burned city, with no linen for its four or five beds, no monitoring equipment, and no heating or cooling system. When sick babies came in, the ICU was a room with a small heating/air conditioning unit in the window. Patients had to bring their own linen and food. Medicines and supplies came from Ramadi and often didn't arrive at all. There were no immunizations and some patients could be seen in the plaza getting their chests listened to and having prescriptions written. Most of the public health clinics had been bombed and lay in rubble, and where the shells of those existed, people had stolen the toilets, the electrical wires, everything that could be stripped out of the buildings. That was the medical system Captain John Nadeau saw when he arrived in Haditha, Iraq. But that's not what he saw in his mind. He could picture a functioning system, able to deliver far better health care in clean, functioning environments. He had a vision, a dream, and he decided he would do something about it.

The hospital had been right in the middle of the fighting in the days of Saddam Hussein. "The wing of the hospital that held their kitchen, their laundry, their pharmacy had been blown up and burned during the war," John said. Where they did their surgeries, "the cement from the roof was falling into the operating theater." When he met with the people there and asked how he could help, they told him they wanted office furniture. John told them, "We're not buying office furniture." They wanted a CT scanner. He said, "Look, you are in the middle of nowhere, and you need a basic hospital, not CT scanners. Number one, you don't have a radiologist to read CT scans. You don't have any technicians to run them. You don't have anyone who will support them and they break down all the time. Siemens is not coming to Haditha where their technician might get killed. You don't need a high-tech machine that you can't use."

Just before the war, a high-tech sterilizing machine had been delivered. But it needed compressed air, which they didn't have, and it needed water under pressure, which they didn't have—water came down from the roof by gravity. John would walk the doctors down to the sterilizer that couldn't work. He would point at the nice but useless-in-its-context machine sitting there and he'd say, "This is what your CT scanner will be like. You're not ready for this. Why don't we talk about what basic things you need to get your hospital up and running so you can actually look after people and provide basic health-care services?"

You no doubt get the impression that John was a "keep it real" sort of dreamer. He says, "We, in fact, designed a basic, no-frills hospital, and spent a lot of time with the doctors working on the blueprint." As for the clinics, he left Iraq a better place there, too. "I went out and hired an Iraqi engineer, and he and I went out and we built two clinics before I left," he said, "we got them running, we got the watering system to work, we got electricity, we painted them, we cleaned them up, and we got them working again."

There you have it, from dream to completion. It was the same for Major Kevin Jarrard, who saw a little girl turning blue, gasping, who could barely make it across the room. Yet he dared to picture this terminally ill child well, and between the span of December of 2007 and March of 2008, that happened. A healthy, mischievous, grinning girl came home to Iraq. It was that image that drove him to send a flurry of e-mails to Kelly Jarrard, Janet Jarrard, and Jonathan Malloch when hope for getting Amenah to America sputtered at times.

The depth of dreams has inspired individuals, nations, and generations. Most famously, Dr. Martin Luther King, Jr., had a dream, which became a powerful vision and changed the behavior of an entire country. We all have dreams, goals, and aspirations that motivate us throughout our lives and determine the path we take. These dreams guide us in what we choose to do and when we choose to do it.

Your dream might be better work-life balance, financial security, or a genuinely happy family. Think about dreams that are important to you, get some paper and a pen, find a quiet place, and ask yourself why. For example, if you are highly motivated to be successful in your career, ask, "Why is this important to me?" Write down your answers, then dig a little deeper, and ask again. Your answers might center on financial needs, recognition, achievement, helping others, or the ability to see the world. Don't filter what you write because the answers are important only to you. The point is, if you are spending 60 hours a week at work (your behavior) and you are doing it because you want a successful career (your dream), make sure you know why you want a successful career.

Getting clear about what matters most to you, really understanding your dreams and your values, is essential because dreams determine the direction of your behavior. The ability to step back and take perspective is possible only if there is a solid bedrock of values and vision to stand on. If your dreams aren't clear, your direction won't be clear. It will be left, right, no left again. To fully leverage your thinking skills, you need to know, at the core, what is important in your life and what's not. Thinking and feeling work better together when your dreams are clear and consistent.

Feelings

Ah, emotions. How they make your life worth living! And how they can just as readily get in your way.

You have probably experienced the emotional reaction of losing your cool or blowing up, and then after calming down saying to yourself, "What was I thinking?" The answer is that there probably wasn't much thought going on at all because feelings were in your driver's seat.

When feelings are positive, they drive us. Kevin Jarrard's first look at Amenah was a tug at his heart that made him want to take action—it initiated a dream of a well and healthy Amenah, something that came to pass.

Feelings create momentum and speed, which is necessary to go forward and take action. Remember the first time you fell in love? It was exhilarating, intoxicating, and all consuming. You had butterflies in your stomach, your heart beat faster, and your body tingled. It was a wonderful experience. That single emotion pushed your behavior—powerfully drove your behavior—in many different ways, but most notably toward the person you loved. Yet, feelings can be very powerful, and like an untamed horse, hard to ride.

Emotions can better help you achieve a dream when they are under control, which is easy to say but hard to do. Think of how the rational leader Lieutenant Colonel David Bellon acted when one of his hand-picked men, Kevin Jarrard, came to him with a mission that was driven by emotion. It helped that Kevin had given the matter considerable thought, and had consulted with Nadeau, known to be a careful and systematic thinker.

David Bellon was no stranger to emotional issues. When soldiers are in the heated line of duty, emotions can be very near the surface. When the soldiers go home to America after their duty, they have to act civilly, in control of their emotions. Bellon knew they needed to be just as in charge of their emotions while in Iraq. In fact, that was part of his vision, his dream.

When he recently discussed the state of mind he was in that caused him to encourage Jarrard in his Amenah quest, he said he knew he needed to train his soldiers to deal with their feelings, so they would make the right decisions in emotionally charged situations. He described how feelings can flash when a young Marine is on patrol, as he put it, "those moments when you're enraged, but you still conduct yourself with measured discipline and compassion."

Bellon and Mark Lamelza shared that dream: to take a group of young men through an experience that was probably going to be violent and traumatic and to return them back to their families and their communities as better husbands, fathers, brothers, and citizens. David's two prior tours had been tough—losing young men and women to death and life-altering injuries. In his third tour, he wanted—he needed—to make sure that every soldier had moral clarity. He and Mark spent a lot of time indoctrinating the soldiers with a clear message of "who we are." Somewhere in the future, David said, he didn't want one of his soldiers sitting in a coffeehouse someplace in Palo Alto experiencing angst over "who we were." Instead, he and Mark were determined that the battalion was going to step into this endeavor with moral certainty, quite confident about "who we are and how much we can take." David and Mark's dream reverberated through the 3rd battalion and, undoubtedly, guided the behaviors of every single Marine.

This stance, to take the moral high ground when possible, is in large part behind the impetus to allow Kevin Jarrard to start the chain of seemingly impossible events that resulted in Amenah returning to her home in Iraq healed. And, because the Marine mission at the time was to shift control of the country back to the Iraqi people, to bond with them, to interact with them, this turned out to be a very sage, emotionally driven dream to encourage. As

Nadeau put it, "We got more traction from helping that little girl with the people of Haditha than probably anything else we did."

Feelings do not need to be at the intensity level of rage to override thinking and influence our behavior. A study done by neuroscientist Alan Sanfey at the University of Arizona illustrates the point.[1] The study used a simple negotiation game in which one player has to split $10 with a second player. In this game, let's say Jane is the first player and Joe is the second player.

Jane can offer Joe any amount, from zero to $10, and she can keep the change, but only if Joe accepts the offer. If Joe rejects the offer, neither of them gets any money.

According to game theory and common sense, Joe should accept the offer no matter how low it is because getting some money is better than getting no money. That is rational, reward-driven behavior, right? Well, it doesn't work that way. Here is what happens. As the offer gets down to a couple of dollars, the people in Joe's role consistently turn down the offer and forego the free money. If you put yourself in Joe's shoes, you know the reason—people get mad at cheapskate offers, and would rather have nothing than a couple of dollars.

The really interesting part of this research is that the investigators mapped the brain of the players while they were playing. As the offers became increasingly unfair, a region in the brain that is tied to negative emotions, such as anger and disgust, became more active. When this region became more active than the region in the brain that drives goal-oriented reasoning, players rejected the offer. Feelings overruled thinking and sent a resounding message: "You cheap jerk. If you can't be fair, then you'll lose, even if it costs me, too." You might be inclined to attribute the rejected offer to principle or sense of fair play, but magnetic imaging suggests that feelings drove behavior.

Let's take one last look at feelings that are so subtle we don't even recognize their occurrence, but they still impact behavior. This example is a Gordian knot. Social science research consistently shows that we have a tendency to fear people who are different from ourselves. We might not think of ourselves as prejudiced, but at a physiological level, we do show a fear reaction to people who are different from ourselves. Indiscriminant evolutionary cues are signaling us that different means dangerous. We wouldn't recognize the feeling as fear, but instead might draw a gut conclusion that we don't like the person. In a global world that is becoming closer each day, people need to be aware of unconscious biases like this. The way to cut the Gordian knot is to recognize that feelings operate in this fashion.

When feelings row much harder and faster than thinking, it creates an imbalance, and you typically have trouble making good judgments. That doesn't mean you should try to repress your feelings as if they were Victorian-era vices. That won't work—they just won't behave, so the best practice is to recognize your feelings and the important role they play so that they work for you and are in concert with your thinking.

Thinking

For someone like Jonathan Malloch, thinking is a regular day at work and a way of life. He had to find the safest, yet most affordable way to get Amenah to and from America with minimal risk to his colleagues. Chartering a Galaxy 6 or hiring the air medical agencies was out of financial reach, no matter how energetically Janet and Kelly were gathering donations. This is someone who charts every step of a process and has contingent plans B and C for each step. He had to deal with the state department, which offered little real support and basically said, "We know you're coming. Just don't mess this up." He had to study and rehearse all the Muslim custom issues with his extraction team colleagues. And he was ready to pull the plug on his team's involvement if the risk grew too great, which it did at one point until Blackwater Worldwide agreed to help escort the team.

Aside from tournament chess players, few people have to study as many permutations of a situation as Jonathan did. But thinking, when powered by your dreams and feelings, can be a very powerful aspect of your life.

Thinking is the third member of the rowing team, and building thinking skills is what this book is really about. Thanks to your thinking side, you can anticipate, plan, invent, innovate, contemplate, and decide. On a daily basis, when you are sizing up situations, gathering information, weighing alternatives, and considering consequences, you are using this marvelous side of your mind. Its capabilities are boundless, so you can continually get better at thinking. From an evolutionary perspective, reasoned reflective thinking developed fairly recently and is housed in the newest part of our brain, and like a shiny new computer, it can process a lot of information and purposefully drive behavior. Thinking plays a key role in recognizing and evaluating life-changing opportunities, solving complicated problems, and making wise decisions.

Another role of thinking is to act as an emergency brake when feelings run too fast. The connection between primitive feelings and behavior tends to occur very quickly, so in this situation the key on the thinking side is to be able to rapidly recognize and label those feelings. It is a reactive position, analogous to an emergency situation where rapid recognition and response is necessary. The purpose is to gain a foothold and interrupt the flow of emotion. Of course, the majority of situations in our daily lives are more mundane and thinking can and should play a proactive role in how we behave. Accessing your thinking side across everyday situations will greatly enhance your life, allowing you to be in control, shaping intentional behavior, and moving in a positive direction.

Developing your thinking will also give you a highly sought-after skill that is in short supply. Employers and educators in our country are waving red flags because employees and students are not demonstrating the kind of thinking it takes to meet the demands of a rapidly changing world that requires responsiveness and independent judgment. A nationwide survey of employers highlights the extent of the problem; among employees new to the workforce, under 30 percent of those with a college degree, only 4 percent of those with a two-year degree, and none of those with a high school degree were rated as possessing excellent critical thinking skills.[2] Those numbers suggest a gap between capabilities and demands that needs to close to sustain societal well-being and prosperity.

As you can see from Amenah's story, good thinking can shape miracles, or support them as they unfold. By developing your thinking, you can position yourself to meet the demands of a complex world, and, in turn, you can use your newfound talent to positively impact the world with inspired dreams and dedicated achievements.

Summary

In this chapter, you put the pieces together, learning why people behave the way they do and how dreams, thoughts, and feelings work together to determine our actions and behaviors. Understanding how your mind works is critical at that very moment when you are about to act and you need to decide if thinking or feelings will run the show. You need clear dreams so that you have a road map that points you in the right direction. Understanding how your feelings work allows you to use them to your advantage. They are like an eccentric family member—you love them and need them even though they embarrass you from time to time—so it's best to acknowledge their existence and get to know them well. And finally, thinking is your ace in the hole. It is an unlimited resource that you can harness to improve the quality of your life and the lives of those around you.

Endnotes and References

1. Sanfey, Alan G., J. K. Rilling, J. A. Aronson, L. E. Nystrom, and J. D. Cohen. 2003. The neural basis of economic decision-making in the ultimatum game. *Science* 300:1755–58.

2. *Are They Really Ready to Work? Employers Perspectives on the Basic Knowledge and Applied Skills of New Entrants to the 21st Century US Workforce.* 2006. Study conducted by The Conference Board, Partnership for 21st Century Skills, Corporate Voices for Working Families, and the Society for Human Resource Management.

Damasio, Antonio. 1994. *Descartes' error: Emotion, reason, and the human brain.* New York: Avon Books.

A New Way of Thinking

Jonathan Malloch made numerous calls and sat down several times with the extraction team of Glenn Susskind and Gary White as they scrutinized lists, charts, and cost sheets to determine the feasibility and best ways of transporting Amenah to Nashville. As Gary put it, "You don't just hop on a plane and run over to Iraq and bring a girl back." There were a lot of moving parts to consider, so they went to work, identifying the most crucial questions: Could the child fly, did they have the logistic ability to get from the Iraq border to Amman, what type of air transportation was needed (e.g., air ambulance), what type of transportation was possible given the costs, how would they transport their medical equipment through international airport security, and how would they secure an interpreter?

They didn't waste time with irrelevant questions, and they didn't overlook a single crucial detail or possibility as they assessed risks, probabilities, and options. They were expert thinkers in this arena, all having served professionally as part of the Disaster Medical Assistance Team, which is now housed under the Department of Health and Human Services. Their experience and expertise came from working together in crisis situations, such as the immediate aftermath of Hurricane Katrina. Some of their expertise had to do with their medical background and training, but their experience also came from having to think through emergency situations; to work effectively with ambiguous, inconsistent, and incomplete information; to make the best possible judgments given the circumstances; and to plan effectively under time pressures.

An expert in any field learns to organize and group information around principles. That allows the expert to quickly draw information when he or she needs it. Doctors see a symptom, scan through a database in their heads, and ask a series of questions to quickly winnow down the possible causes. Peyton Manning can scan a football field, see opportunities and risks, and make snap decisions with great success. A novice organizes information in a more random and error-prone fashion. By putting a thinking model in your head, you are organizing important steps and information, which helps you learn more quickly and efficiently. A model, like a recipe, helps you see the ingredients and steps for success. So, let's look at five steps of a model that can become a valuable part of your own thinking.

Five Steps to New Thinking

1. Stop and Think

After David Bellon listened to Kevin Jarrard's proposal, he walked back to the base, which took about an hour. He thought about Kevin—was he on his game? He thought about Dr. Nadeau and the expertise he brought to the situation, their mission in Haditha, and his and Mark's dream of moral certainty for their soldiers. He processed and he reflected in the solitude of the night. By the time he arrived at the base, he had sized up the situation, knew what his next steps would be, and anticipated that his role would be one of strategy and influence with higher command.

Janet Jarrard, Kevin's aunt back in Tennessee, was a PR specialist. But she was faced with an unusual conundrum. She needed to solicit funds to finance the transportation of Amenah, her mother, an extraction team, as well as a female escort. But she couldn't use any of the best tools of public relations. She couldn't initiate a media event able to garner attention and funds, nor could she use any of the latest social media tools, all of which could make her task far easier. If word got out too soon, Amenah and her mother might never make it out of Iraq. Their lives would be at risk. She'd also been asked to organize the medical extraction team and help find a female escort for the mother and sick child. So Janet had to pause and consider possibilities. It was all daunting, and some of it was a little over her head. What could she do? How could she go about all of this, yet do it in the quietest and most effective way possible?

When faced with the impossible, it's often best to start with the small steps of what is possible. Once she weighed her options, a quiet e-mail flurry to all her friends and acquaintances seemed the only real way to start a grassroots fire able to sweep in funds and solicit help with the harder parts of the mission. In time, the pieces began to fall into place. Her friend Lisa Van Wye, a nurse from Bowling Green, Kentucky, offered to be the female escort from Jordan to the states. Deanna Dolan, of World Relief, rounded up an interpreter and led Janet to the Bergers, who offered their home as a place to stay, while the Grace Chapel Church in Lieper's Fork, Tennessee, started to help gather funds. And, pivotal to the most daunting task of all, Jonathan Malloch got in touch with her and said, "What can I do?" That completed the missing parts of the puzzle as the impossible, in the way of such miracles, started to look pretty darn doable.

Being able to stop and think is a reflective skill; it is the ability to stop and figure out what type of thinking skill you need at this point in time. When you do this, you are actively taking control of your thinking. The situation might be life changing, an unproductive debate with your teenager, a problem at work, or an entrepreneurial opportunity. The situation does not matter—the process remains the same. You stop and think about your thinking so that you can apply the correct strategy for the situation. Here are a few simple, but essential reflective questions to ask yourself:

- What is going on here (or with me)? Stop and define the situation and gauge your feelings. Notice that the first step for both Lieutenant Colonel Bellon and Gary White was to "size up the situation."

- What am I (are we) trying to accomplish? Stop and define your purpose or goal. Keeping your purpose, goal, or dream at the forefront prevents derailment and keeps feelings in check.

- What type of situation is this? Stop and figure out if it is urgent or important. Most situations are not urgent or extremely important. When they are, you want to be ready to apply your thinking skills. When they aren't, you don't want to waste energy by treating them like they are.

- Do I need to know more? Determine if you need more information to answer what (facts), when, why (the context), or how (process) questions. Do you need more information to determine if there is a need to plan, to monitor, or to evaluate?

By thinking reflectively, you put yourself in a position to identify the real problem, or put small problems in perspective so that you don't waste valuable time and energy. Asking yourself reflective questions improves your awareness and focuses your thinking. It allows you to apply what you already know to the situation at hand.

Learn to Stop and Think

The best way to become better at stopping and thinking is to pick one activity, for example, meetings at work or the times when you review your finances. Choose any situation where you want to think more deeply. As you approach the situation, stop and ask a few reflective questions. (For example: What am I trying to accomplish? Which thinking style would be most helpful here? What is my emotional temperature right now?) Don't rush your answers; give yourself time to process a thoughtful response.

It is more challenging to stop and think when the stakes are high. When a big decision is on the table or a conflict is in play, feelings often come to the forefront and exert too much influence. One way to prepare for these high-pressure moments is to set aside time to think about a significant or emotional moment that occurred previously in your life. Run instant replay; play that moment in your head like a motion picture. Mentally pause the picture and ask yourself reflective questions. You are not trying to change the past, but instead you want to rehearse and practice new thinking at the right moment. Using a past event is a safe way to practice so that you can prepare to do it successfully when the next big situation arises. You are cueing and rehearsing so that you will be ready.

2. Recognize Assumptions[1]

If you go to the Ritz Carlton, you'll get great customer service and if you buy a Honda, it will be a reliable car. These are common assumptions based on the reputation of the companies. Assumptions, statements, or beliefs that you assume to be true operate almost automatically, so you take them for granted without checking the facts. They are useful because they save you time. If you didn't make assumptions, you would be forever checking every single fact in every single instance. In essence, you would be repeatedly and forever saying, "How do I know that to be true?" Your life would grind to a halt.

The problem with assumptions is that sometimes they are wrong. Not too long ago, leading fashion retailer Gap Inc. decided to launch a new logo to refresh its brand. The old logo had been in place for decades and the company assumed a more contemporary image was needed. Unfortunately, it didn't check its assumption and the online community condemned the move. After only one week, Gap Inc. recalled the new logo and brought back the old one. When assumptions are wrong, they send you down a dead-end track, and you don't even know you are heading in the wrong direction, which can be a costly mistake. The ability to recognize assumptions will help you avoid pitfalls, and the best place to start is to understand where assumptions come from.

Personal experience is the most common source of an assumption and it is the most difficult to recognize. We hold beliefs and make assumptions based on our culture, background, and experience. Do you favor health-care reform? Do you know why you hold this belief? We see through the eyes of our own experience, and we don't know what we don't know.

Gary White, Glenn Susskind, and Lisa Van Wye prepared for their trip to the Iraq border by reviewing a culture brief that was prepared by the Department of Navy Intelligence. They reviewed proper protocol related to religious and cultural practices in the region and specifically within Amenah's tribe. They received an additional briefing, courtesy of Blackwater Worldwide, on how to prepare for the trip from the Iraq border to Amman, including how to dress, how to comb their hair, and how to avoid unexpected behaviors. Any assumption based on their American experience might cause a problem in a situation that had no room for error. They were American civilians and this was dangerous terrain for them. Furthermore, they would be dealing with a sick toddler who did not speak English, and they didn't want to do anything that might unnecessarily upset her. A fear-based tantrum or agitation would drain precious oxygen that she couldn't afford to waste.

Learn to Recognize Assumptions

Distinguish fact from opinion. That isn't as easy as it looks. When you hear someone say, "Macs are easier to use than PCs," do you nod in agreement? Most of us do, but that statement is an opinion that needs to be tested (e.g., by asking for whom and in which applications). Popular opinions are the tricky ones, so see how good you can become at distinguishing facts and opinions as you listen to people, watch the news, and surf the Internet. The ability to distinguish facts from opinions will help you recognize assumptions.

Identify stated versus unstated assumptions. Stated assumptions are explicit and you see them all of the time in project plans and contracts: "Josh can complete the project in two weeks, assuming he works full-time on the project." By stating the assumption, everyone knows what is required (he won't be able to work on anything else). Stating assumptions increases clarity, quantifies risk, and is a good way to manage your workload.

Unstated assumptions are where trouble usually begins. In dating relationships, couples sometimes hold very different assumptions about what it means to "be together" or to "take a break." Romantic comedies bank on this type of misunderstanding and miscommunication. Unstated assumptions run rampant in projects and financial deals gone awry and their consequences can be serious.

Most of the volunteers in "Amenah's Story," with the exception of Jonathan Malloch, did not really understand the complexity associated with one very short portion of the trip—the 280 miles between Amman, Jordan, and the Iraq border. They assumed it would be difficult, but they had no idea how difficult. For example, there were numerous checkpoints along the road between Amman and the border, each with long lines of vehicles waiting to pass through the checkpoint. Glenn noted that they hadn't anticipated this event because it is not something you see in America. They had assumed a more expedient route, and, thankfully, their Blackwater escort was able to bypass the lines. Glenn acknowledged that extra hours going through checkpoints would have made it virtually impossible for them to keep Amenah stable without depleting their medical supplies on the first part of the journey.

The Marines weren't anticipating near-blizzard conditions as Kevin and the family flew from Haditha to the Iraqi border. It was an extremely unusual event, and military people serving in the region at that time often refer to this January day in 2008 as "the day it snowed in the desert." Understandably, the Marines had assumed that weather conditions would be within a normal range for the region, and had not planned for delays that extreme weather can cause. Fortunately, this unstated assumption did not derail the project, but weather did come close to shutting down their transportation plans.

It is not easy to recognize unstated assumptions, so we invite you to practice. Can you identify the unstated assumption in this statement? "We need a better recycling program at work. It is important to increase awareness of green initiatives in our company." Think about what is being implied. The unstated assumption is that a better recycling program will increase awareness. Once you recognize an assumption, you can evaluate it. Maybe a better recycling program will increase awareness, maybe it won't, or maybe something else would be more effective. If you state the assumption (I assume that a better recycling program will increase awareness of green initiatives at work), you are more likely to evaluate it correctly.

3. Evaluate Information

Before you can jump on an opportunity, you need to evaluate its merits. When you are trying to choose between alternatives, you need to sort through their relative strengths and weaknesses. To make a good choice, you need to evaluate information. The good news is that information is far more accessible than it used to be. The bad news is that our society is now swimming in a sea of information and misinformation. It can feel overwhelming, and to cope effectively, you need a systematic approach.

Before evaluating information, be sure you clarify the situation (stop and think) so that you know what's going on, what you are trying to accomplish, and what type of situation it is. This helps you determine how much and what type of information to gather and evaluate. Try to root out vague and ambiguous language. When you hear phrases like, "I just want to be happy" or "we want a win-win outcome," you've got vague and ambiguous goals. Clarify before you move forward. It takes time to gather information, so know what you need to look for (and what you don't) before you start.

Is It Relevant and Accurate?

What did Janet Jarrard, Jonathan Malloch, and Mark Lamelza have in common, besides their shared goal to help Amenah? They each needed to clearly describe what success would look like so they could gather and evaluate the right information. For Janet, the keys to success were related to adequate funding and resources (e.g., to pay for airline tickets, to secure housing, to get a female escort, to locate a female interpreter in Nashville). For Jonathan, it was the safety of the civilian medical team and their patient. For Mark Lamelza, it was maintaining security and governance operations in the region without disruption. To evaluate information, you need to have a framework around which you can organize the information. Janet, Jonathan, and Mark each started with criteria that allowed them to efficiently evaluate information related to their part of the operation.

As soon as you have criteria or a "keys for success" checklist in place, you can use two simple questions to evaluate information. The first question centers on the relevance of the information. Sometimes people get off track sorting through irrelevant information, and the common consequence is to feel overwhelmed or confused. As you review information, you will want to ask yourself, over and over again, "Is it relevant based on my keys for success?"

Kevin and his colleagues needed to get tribal permission for Amenah and her mother to travel to America and there were several different groups in Haditha trying to influence the outcome. Rumors floated around and Kevin and his colleagues certainly needed to be aware of political influences, but they couldn't keep tabs on all of the information that was bubbling up. They needed to determine which information was relevant and which wasn't, so they focused on the person who would ultimately make the decision, the tribal sheik. They evaluated information related to the al-Jughayfi tribe's Sheik Said Flayah Othman's viewpoint, trying to be fully aware of what the sheik knew and what he considered important because he could give the go-ahead. They directed their precious time and attention toward evaluating the information that mattered most.

Now let's go to the second simple question: Is it accurate? Be on the lookout for information that sounds accurate, but is vague. Notice the difference between "Doctors recommend Zymbia." and "A survey of the American Medical Association showed that 87 percent of the doctors surveyed recommended Zymbia." It is easier to evaluate the accuracy of the second example. Watch out for popular opinions (e.g., Macs are easier to use than PCs). They might be accurate, but also be vague regarding for whom and when the conditions are true.

Consider the medical information on Amenah that the extraction planning team was receiving from Iraq. As they prepared for their trip overseas, they would get snippets of information, often through second- and thirdhand sources. The initial reports indicated that she was in reasonably good shape. However, they needed to prepare for arduous travel and they could not confirm the accuracy of the medical information they were receiving. They contacted Dr. Doyle, a pediatric cardiologist at Vanderbilt, several times to go over the information they were receiving, and to collectively work through possible implications. But in the end, they knew that it would be dangerous to take the information they had at face value. Instead, they prepared for medical scenarios that ranged from a relatively healthy child with a hole in her heart to a worst-case scenario. Not accepting information at face value proved to be a wise decision because they were prepared when they met a very sick little girl.

It is also important to look at the source of the information when evaluating accuracy. For example, do you think Wikipedia is a credible source? How do you know? To gauge the credibility of a source, ask questions: Does the source have expertise in this area? Is his or her expertise up to date? Is he or she impartial and trustworthy? It is important to check your sources.

Jonathan Malloch was getting ready to call off the mission because he had received information from several sources that the operation couldn't be done. He needed to make a decision, but before he did, he called Gary White and asked for his thoughts. He hesitated for the safety of his colleagues uppermost, even though Blackwater had assured him they could help orchestrate the extraction. Gary told him that he needed to listen to the people who had frontline experience. He said, "Jonathan, you need to listen to the people in the trenches, those are the ones who know it more than someone who is four or five hundred miles away sitting behind a desk. I don't mean to be disrespectful, but it's just the truth." Gary and Glenn thought the mission could be accomplished, and Jonathan respected and trusted their input.

Am I Being Persuaded?

Sometimes when you are evaluating information, others will try to actively shape your evaluation. Persuasion is used successfully by leaders, salespeople, marketing specialists, and even our children to influence and motivate. Being aware of persuasion techniques helps you sort out relevant and accurate information from fluff and spin.

Some persuasion techniques are fairly obvious, such as using a respected person as a spokesperson or using emotionally charged language and appealing to human dreams and desires. Others are more subtle, as evidenced in drug company commercials. Some drug commercials leverage the fact that most people can only remember six to eight pieces of information at a time, and information that is presented first and last is remembered best. The commercials present a long list of benefits, followed by risks and side effects, and then benefits again. Research[2] has shown that benefits are sometimes presented using words that are easier to understand and are presented at a slower speed than the risks and side effects, and sometimes visual distraction is added to the mix. The end result of this careful orchestration is that people remember the benefits, but have difficulty remembering the risks and side effects. Training (such as learning to ask questions about relevancy and accuracy) helps you counteract persuasion techniques and improves your ability to evaluate information.

Am I Being Objective?

When you are evaluating information, you can also get sidetracked by common cognitive biases. Human brains tend to use heuristics, simple rules that increase efficiency but introduce systematic error. A number of these mind traps are described in Appendix B,

"Cognitive Biases: Common Mental Mind Traps," but here is a flavor of how they work. If you hear that 92 percent of the patients with a certain disease survive an illness, you will view that information more favorably than if you hear that 8 percent of the patients die. The odds are the same, but you evaluate differently based on the way the information is framed.

Even more pervasive is confirmation bias, the tendency to remember and agree with information that is consistent with your beliefs and values and to not seek out or to critically review information that does match your beliefs. On the morning that Pearl Harbor was bombed, the incoming Japanese planes were spotted on radar and reported, but no action was taken. American planes were due in that day and no one really believed that an attack like that was possible. Confirmation bias happens to all of us, and one way to minimize it, and other cognitive biases, is to add a third question: Am I being objective? Through this question, you are pausing to look more carefully at what you are seeing or hearing.

4. Draw Conclusions

Making the right decision can change your life. It might be making that instantaneous connection in a single moment, or choosing from multiple alternatives after thoughtful contemplation, that forever shifts your life's course. Either way, the sequence is the same; you accurately evaluate the information and draw a conclusion that logically follows from the information. Unfortunately, mistakes often occur at the intersection between evaluating information and drawing conclusions. Let's look at two common mistakes:

- *Jumping to conclusions* often occurs when people are under pressure to move quickly or when they are very results driven. Workplaces across America reward people who take action and get results, and the one downside is a nationwide tendency to jump on the first conclusion without fully vetting other possibilities.

Certainly, the Marines in Operation Amenah were both action oriented and under intense time pressure. However, as a part of their training, they have been taught how to quickly develop and evaluate multiple options before drawing a conclusion. In combat situations, jumping to conclusions can have deadly consequences. In independent interviews, Kevin Jarrard, David Bellon, and Mark Lamelza each consistently described how they canvassed options before drawing a conclusion; this skill is ingrained in these men.

■ *Overgeneralization* is also common, and it occurs when you draw a conclusion that goes well beyond the information at hand. Would you invest all of your savings in the stock market because you read a favorable article in the *Financial Times*? Of course not. Yet, the economic road over the last few years is scattered with the carcasses of organizations that made a practice of drawing conclusions that extended far beyond a base of solid information.

When Lieutenant Colonel Bellon received permission from higher headquarters for Kevin and colleagues to proceed, he knew the parameters of that approval; there was no room for overgeneralization. He accurately concluded that permission was tenuous at best, and any action that diverted attention from their official mission would result in a quick reversal of the decision.

Inductive and Deductive Reasoning

Let's look at the process of drawing a conclusion now that we have seen how a couple of common miscues occur. To understand how you draw conclusions, you need to know about deductive and inductive reasoning. To help you, pick a detective from your favorite crime-solving show (e.g., *NCIS, The Mentalist, CSI, Sherlock Holmes*)—any one will do. Here is the story:

A woman was shot, her body was found in her apartment, and her boyfriend is the primary suspect. At the time of death, he was with some buddies at a local bar two blocks from her apartment. However, he left the bar for ten minutes to get something from his car, and no one noticed him while he was gone. If the woman was murdered in her apartment, the boyfriend had sufficient time to commit the crime. However, your favorite detective (insert name here) thinks she was murdered across town. If so, the boyfriend could not have shot her.

This "if so" logic is deductive reasoning. If something is true (she died on the other side of town), then certain conclusions can be deduced (the boyfriend was not with her when she died). In deductive reasoning, you use a "top down" approach. Principles and laws are applied (e.g., you can't be in two different places at the same time) to draw a conclusion. Applying proven principles, rules, and laws to move from information to conclusion reduces error and adds rigor to your thinking.

When Glenn Susskind was trying to determine the oxygen supply required for the trip, he noted that Amenah lived in low country, not the mountains. So, he assumed that she was near sea level and that her blood was only semioxygenated because of her illness. He knew that the type of plane required to make the trip would pressurize at 8,000 feet. Glenn was using deductive reasoning and applying laws of physics to estimate her oxygen needs during the flight.

Inductive reasoning is more of a "bottom up" approach in which observations are made that lead to a conclusion. When your favorite detective arrived on the scene, he or she closely examined the body, then stepped back and said, "She wasn't killed here. She probably died on the beach." The detective noticed sand under her fingernails, the scent of seaweed, and no blood on the carpet. Based on these observations, the detective inferred that she died elsewhere, probably at the beach on the other side of town. The detective can't be sure, but it is an educated guess. In inductive reasoning, you connect a set of observations to make an educated guess about how they are related. Inductive reasoning is useful when you are trying to identify patterns and trends.

Dr. Nadeau observed the current state of the local hospital in Haditha, which had been crippled by war. He reviewed a U.S. government contract that proposed spending $2.5 million on restoring the hospital. He also reviewed the types of resources that the local doctors were requesting, which did not match basic medical needs. He then sat down and reviewed what the local infrastructure could support and the common medical needs of the people in Haditha. When he connected the dots, he knew that the 2.5 million dollars would be wasted. Dr. Nadeau was using inductive reasoning when he drew this conclusion, and also when he proposed rebuilding a basic hospital that would be suited for the needs of the people and supportable with current infrastructure.

Good decision making (or problem solving) is about drawing conclusions that logically follow from accurate and relevant information. You use deductive and inductive reasoning skills to make the connection between information and conclusion. When the connection slips (e.g., jumping to conclusions, overgeneralizing), so does the quality of the decision.

5. Develop a Plan of Action

Once a decision is made, what happens next? A plan of action helps you anticipate consequences and brings your decision to life. The type of planning needed depends, to a certain extent, on the type of decision (e.g., project plan, business plan, wedding plan). However, when you move from decision to action, three questions will get you off to a good start:

- What are the consequences of this decision?
- What plans need to be made to implement this decision?
- What types of resources are needed to implement this decision?

In "Amenah's Story," there were multiple action plans, and each was very detailed and specific. That level of detail was necessary to successfully orchestrate a complex life-and-death mission. Of course, most decisions will not require this level of planning, but it is important to remember that a decision is the beginning, not the end point. Leveraging the qualities of a timely style helps to bring a proactive, resourceful approach to bear on a plan of action. Similarly, using an analytical style and looking for inconsistencies or missing pieces of the plan helps avoid gaffes and miscues. A plan of action keeps you focused, helps you avoid unnecessary detours, and leads to more predictable and promising outcomes.

Summary

Every day, you are bombarded with information and you will absorb it differently than you did before. Perhaps you will notice an opinion that looks like a fact, recognize an unstated assumption, or catch yourself agreeing with something just because it matches your beliefs. Maybe you will quickly recognize irrelevant information and save yourself time by moving on to something more relevant. Maybe you will see similarities across pieces of information and connect the dots using inductive reasoning. Regardless of what you learned in this chapter, the end result is that you are thinking differently.

You now have a new model for thinking and a series of relevant questions that allows you to organize your thoughts as you approach opportunities, problems, and decisions. The five-step model helps you approach thinking more like an expert (organizing and grouping information, asking better questions) than a novice. Practice your new skills each day, and you will quickly see positive results.

Endnotes

1. A New of Way Thinking is based on Pearson's RED model of critical thinking (www.ThinkWatson.com). The RED model (Recognize Assumptions, Evaluate Arguments, and Draw Conclusions) stems

from more than 85 years of research on critical thinking. This program of research is based primarily on the Watson-Glaser™ II Critical Thinking Appraisal, a leading assessment of critical thinking ability.

2. Professor Ruth S. Day of Duke University leads a program of cognitive research, including cognitive accessibility of drug benefits and risks. Her research is summarized on her faculty Web page at www.duke.edu.

Take Stock of Your Style

On the flip side of the details and events of "Amenah's Story," where everyone had their approriate thinking caps on and played to their particular styles and strengths, sometimes (often) events do not play out so smoothly.

Following the January 12, 2010, earthquake that devastated Haiti, a bus pulled up to a checkpoint on the Dominican Republic. Inside were 33 children, aged from 2 to 12, who were being escorted by a group of ten Baptist missionaries. Instead of being passed through the check station, the children were taken off in one direction by authorities and the missionaries were taken in another direction and arrested on January 29 for kidnapping.

Laura Silsby, of Meridian, Idaho, who led the nine other members of the missionary group, told the media she was only trying to save suffering children. However, there were a few details she had not even shared with her fellow missionaries:

- An areawide concern about human trafficking had made authorities exceptionally sensitive to the movement of people out of Haiti by anyone.

- Many of the children being transported were not even orphans. At least 20 of the children were from a single village and had living parents. Some of the parents told the AP they willingly turned over their children to the missionaries on

- the promise the Americans would educate them and allow relatives to visit.

- Silsby had decided the previous summer to create an orphanage in the Dominican Republic, and in November of 2009, she registered the nonprofit New Life Children's Refuge foundation in Idaho. After Haiti's catastrophic earthquake, she accelerated the plan and recruited her fellow missionaries.

- A Dominican diplomat who said Laura had visited him the same day the missionaries tried to take the children out of the country told the AP that he had warned her that without the proper papers, she could be arrested.

So, surprise, surprise, things went wrong at the border and the well-intentioned group was arrested.

As someone getting a clearer look at how good thinking works, you can, no doubt, spot a few errors in the thinking style in this situation. Now, contrast and compare that event with how smoothly Amenah's situation went, in spite of numerous obstacles and adjustments.

Major Kevin Jarrard's Good Samaritan background could have led him to leap to a decision, but he avoided making any assumptions and wanted to consider all aspects and steps before he took any action. He also played to an array of supportive careful thinkers who, each in his or her own way, helped to turn a difficult and complicated task into a doable one.

Think about a time when you successfully thought through a challenging situation—a time when you did it right and you did it well. Do you remember what you did that led to success? You might even come up with, "not specifically," because you might not have a vocabulary to describe successful thinking. You might have a broad sense of what worked and what didn't. Not knowing your thinking style and how you replicate successes and avoid mistakes could create a rut instead of opening opportunities for new success. If making a pros and cons list worked when you were trying to decide if you wanted to go out on a date with someone in high school, then you are likely to keep using that process to help make decisions. Evaluating pros and cons has become part of your repertoire.

Collecting good techniques as you go along certainly isn't bad, but it is not intentional. Relying on whatever happens to be in your toolkit is not the same as having a full set of tools in a well-organized box. To be successful, really successful, you need to be intentional. You need to know your style and your skills, exactly what they are and how they work for you. The good news is that it is easy to learn.

Let's look at how knowing, cultivating, and shaping positive thinking styles help you become a great thinker. We all possess thinking styles, which are positive habits that support the development of thinking skills. For example, approaching problems by carefully analyzing the situation or looking for facts and important details is a style.

You have preferred thinking styles, which means that you use certain positive behaviors more frequently and across various situations. You can access those behaviors quickly and comfortably. So, you lead with your preferred styles as you build your thinking skills. That is what successful people do—they leverage their strengths.

Understanding Your Thinking Styles

At this point, you are probably saying, "So, how exactly do I figure out my preferred thinking styles?" One option is to take the My Thinking Styles assessment, which is free and takes about 10 minutes to complete (see sidebar). You will receive feedback that describes your preferred thinking styles and how you can use them to your advantage. Each style is positive, and all seven styles contribute in different ways to good thinking. For you, the question is which styles do you use most frequently and comfortably, and which ones are less natural? You might find it easier to relate to the varied thinking styles if you first assess yourself before you explore the styles. Although that might work best for most people, you can also consider the styles that follow and see which one, or which combination of styles, most plays to your thinking strengths.

Assess Your Thinking Styles

Go to www.ThinkWatson.com/mythinkingstyles. It will take you less than 10 minutes to complete the assessment, and it is best to take it when you are not rushed or distracted. Give yourself time to comfortably answer the questions. When you finish, you will receive a personal feedback report that describes your preferred thinking styles.

Analytical Style

Jonathan Malloch had a map on the wall of his office with all of the key players and all of the possible players. He created an algorithm that allowed him to sift through three to five options for every step of the extraction process, so that if one option failed, they could move to the next. At every single point in the plan, they had an alternative option. Jonathan knew that he needed "to get pieces in place in a way that is ironclad." As he explained, "We had a lot of plans that we could have launched with, but none of them were secure. I was unwilling to send this team unless I knew—as much as could be known—that these guys would return safely. I did not want to have a conversation with their wives and their family about why they didn't return." Jonathan knew that he had to prepare for every possibility and to review every detail.

If you are analytical, you like to anticipate consequences and identify strengths and weaknesses in plans. You are quick to think about if-then scenarios and how they might play out. You like to study situations and think about pros and cons. If something doesn't fit in a situation or an important detail is missing, you are likely to notice. You are comfortable studying situations and concentrating on the pieces and how they logically fit together. You are likely to sort through facts and analyze information that is received, rather than just accepting it at face value. Analytical people can be described as clear thinking, orderly, and rational. Having an analytical style helps build specific thinking skills, such as the following:

- Checking the accuracy of information you receive
- Differentiating facts from opinions
- Clarifying situations by questioning ambiguous or vague language
- Noticing missing or inconsistent pieces of a plan
- Analyzing alternatives in an orderly fashion

Inquisitive Style

A top hypertension specialist and Vanderbilt professor, Dr. Nadeau is the expert, the man with the answers. But he is also the man who wonders why and asks the questions that drive new thinking and innovation. Nadeau wondered what they could do to prevent deaths from battlefield injuries, and, with Lieutenant Colonel Bellon's support, that question led to medical training for all the Marines in the battalion. Theirs was the first battalion to receive intensive medical training, teaching each Marine to deal with common problems that lead to deaths on the battlefield, such as how to reduce bleeding from extremity wounds.

Dr. Nadeau left his day-to-day role of caring for patients with heart disease to look after young Marines in a battle zone because, as he said, he "liked the challenge of doing something completely different." He was also committed to figuring out how to help the Iraqis rebuild their health-care system. That's why, when he went out to the public health clinics that had been completely stripped by vandals, he asked "Why don't we hire Iraqis and rebuild these clinics?" That question led to renovated clinics. In the same way, he helped reengineer the hospital and he actively went out into the community to serve the needs of the local people, including the tribal sheik. After Amenah came back cured, he came across other children like her, and asked, "How can we make this happen more frequently?" Thanks to that question, a second child was helped at the University at Charleston and a third in Amman, Jordan. Dr. Nadeau's frequent questions led to his continual learning and to a series of improvements in medical care and medical facilities.

If you have an inquisitive style, you are intellectually curious and like to learn new things about the world. You want to know why things work the way they do and are comfortable probing deeply into subjects. You like to learn about different cultures and people. For you, information is an opportunity to learn. You have a tolerance for ambiguity and complexity because it gives you an opportunity to figure things out. Inquisitive people can be described as curious, alert, and interested in their surrounding world. Having an inquisitive style helps build specific thinking skills, such as the following:

- Clarifying issues or beliefs
- Identifying the root cause of a problem
- Questioning deeply to unearth assumptions or new perspectives
- Asking how and why questions that help evaluate information or alternatives

Insightful Style

What does Kevin Jarrard mean when he says that every one of the decisions he made was "the result of the totality of my experiences throughout everything that had happened to me up to that point in my life"?

His Good Samaritan background could have led him to leap to decisions or make bad judgments, like that missionary group arrested in Haiti on kidnapping charges while trying to move alleged orphans across the border into the Dominican Republic. But Jarrard avoided making any assumptions and wanted to consider all aspects and steps before he took any action.

He was aware of the Marine mission at that time in Iraq, of the willingness of Lieutenant Colonel Bellon to consider a request such as his, of the capabilities of Captain Nadeau, which strengthened his case, of the people back in the States he could count on for help and action, and of what he needed to do to respect the Muslim family members and the tribal leaders. Furthermore, he was able to assemble a big picture that led to a dream that would be hard, but ultimately doable, as it turned out.

If you have an insightful style, you are able to step back and reflect so that you can gain perspective on a situation or problem. You are likely to stand firm on tough issues, if the evidence supports the position, and you will follow though despite obstacles. You tend to see beyond the immediate and you seek clarity. You are capable of being honest with yourself and set a high standard for yourself. Insightful people can be described as prudent, humble, and reflective. Having an insightful style helps build specific thinking skills, such as the following:

- Taking time to reflect
- Maintaining perspective, even in difficult situations
- Willingness to persevere
- Accurately understanding personal strengths and weaknesses
- Making judgments that fit the evidence (don't overgeneralize or oversimplify)

Open-Minded Style

Let's pause to consider again one of the most dynamic aspects of "Amenah's Story." A Muslim child and her mother were being sent to the Christian Bible Belt of America, where they would stay in the home of Christian Pastor Steve Berger and his wife Sarah, be embraced by the church's congregation, have their travel financed from donations all across the area, have their cultural foods and customs respected, and no one would make any attempt to convert them, but rather accept them for who they were and honor them as fellow human beings who needed help.

Following 9/11, some people in America wrote graffiti on and damaged convenience stores owned and operated by members of the American Muslim community. Then, there were people like Pastor Terry Jones from Gainesville, Florida, who burned the Koran in March of 2011, an act that drew angry condemnation in Afghanistan and Pakistan, where anti-American sentiment runs high, causing riots in April in which many people were killed. The actions and emotions of these people mark one extreme of the grassroots mood. There was a lot of confusion and some prejudice about Muslims. Religion can be a very touchy subject, but that was not an issue with all the people who came forward to help.

Deanna Dolan, of World Relief, was one of the first to contact Janet Jarrard and say she wanted to help. One of her key decisions was where to place Amenah and her mother, Maha. She knew her choice was important: "I wanted them to be with people who I trust, people who I know would be committed, and who would be sacrificial. Because it is a huge sacrifice to allow strangers that you've never met, who were coming with huge needs, into your home. I mean, it takes pretty solid people to be able to do that." She weighed the options and chose wisely: Steve and Sarah Berger.

Deanna speaks some Arabic, but she also helped provide Zainab, an interpreter who could help Maha and Amenah communicate. She helped with respect for food and cultural needs, and when she saw fear in the eyes of a mother afraid her child might die on the operating table, she made sure there were people available to support Maha, especially during those stressful hours in the waiting room. She brought together caring Christians from Grace Chapel whose only purpose was to comfort and support a worried mother, one who just happened to be of the Muslim faith. Deanna's approach, though a Christian herself, was to offer support, empathy, and solutions without reservation or judgment.

If you have an open-minded style, you are typically tolerant of the opinions and viewpoints of others and can put yourself in the position of the other person. You can think of different options, different possibilities, and different conclusions. You are comfortable not rushing to judgment, and prefer to thoughtfully weigh information and alternatives. You tend to avoid extreme positions. You value fair play and like to think things through. Open-minded people can be described as intellectually tolerant and fair minded. Having an open-minded style helps build specific thinking skills, such as the following:

- Using an approach that is fair minded
- Seeking information from people with different views or perspectives
- Suspending judgment to evaluate information
- Generating alternative solutions
- Making connections across different situations or topics

Systematic Style

Recall that when David Bellon listened carefully to Kevin Jarrard's proposal, he was assessing Kevin's thinking and putting what he was hearing into context. Kevin's plan was well crafted, but David needed to step back and consider how this plan could affect the larger operation. As he mentally scanned the system, he immediately recognized the challenges and he silently muttered, "Oh, my God, this is going to be a car crash with higher headquarters." He understood that he needed to navigate the system and get buy-in, or at least, avoid the command to stop. He needed to harness relationships that had been developed and protect respect that he had earned from three tours of duty in Iraq. David needed to take a systematic approach in his support of Kevin.

People like Jonathan Malloch, as you saw, can be analytical and systematic when it comes to safety in a well-thought-out plan.

If you are systematic, you are able to size up a situation and place it into context. You are able to see the bigger picture and how the pieces fit together. You approach problems with a logical framework or scheme. You have vision and can anticipate the consequences of different alternatives. Systematic people can be described as conceptual, process oriented, and intuitive. Having a systematic style helps build specific thinking skills, such as the following:

- Comparing perspectives, information, and alternatives
- Developing criteria for evaluating information and alternatives
- Analyzing alternatives
- Making connections across different situations and topics
- Evaluating plans

Timely Style

Few people get bounced a bigger ball that calls for timely action than was Janet Jarrard, Kevin's aunt. When she read the e-mail from Kevin asking her to be the point person in Nashville, she immediately said yes and went to work on December 14th, not knowing exactly what she needed to do, but being fully committed to quickly figuring it out. The time pressure was incredible—a few weeks to secure fund-raising, complete logistical planning, and nail down a multitude of details. Within three days, she had found Jonathan Malloch, and that led to the extraction team being put into place. World Relief, Deanna Dolan, and Grace Chapel church came next. Every single day, she managed to fit another piece of the puzzle into place. Janet describes this time as the most intense period of her life. She didn't know that she could do something like this, but she did. Her efficient, resourceful, and timely approach kept the Nashville side of the operation in sync and moving forward.

Timely people can gather information and make decisions without undue delays. They don't typically get caught up in analysis paralysis or procrastination. Instead, they are able to actively search out relevant information and work their way though situations in a timely manner that is neither too cursory nor too slow. Timely people can be described as efficient, reliable, and responsive. Having a timely style helps develop specific thinking skills, such as the following:

- Being conscientious about working through a problem or opportunity
- Making a timely decision
- Calling for action when it is appropriate
- Appropriately pushing for plans

Truth–Seeking Style

Major Mark Lamelza's job as Operations Officer was to support Lieutenant Colonel Bellon by asking the tough questions and giving honest advice. He said, "The truth is that you always know the right thing to do. The really difficult part of it is actually doing it." Establishing and maintaining local governance, legal systems, and security for the cities in their region all fell under Mark's responsibility. He laughed when he admitted, "I wasn't one of those who jumped on the bandwagon." He knew it was the right thing to do, but he also knew that he had to ask the tough questions and dig deep to make sure that this humanitarian project did not jeopardize anything within the vast umbrella of local governance or security. Mark wasn't naïve; he knew the fragile state of these emerging systems, and he knew that an American-driven plan to move a baby girl and her mother to America for surgery and then back again was risky. Mark's job was to find weaknesses in the plan and then eliminate those weaknesses. He needed to apply a truth-seeking style so that the team could avoid mistakes and recognize potentially dangerous problems.

People who are truth seeking are able to ask tough questions of themselves and others in an effort to get at the truth. They will push deeper for clarity even if it causes some discomfort. They may be skeptical and not willing to accept information at face value. They are not likely to be gullible or passively rely on others for a point of view. Truth seekers can be described as independent, tough minded, and skeptical. Having a truth-seeking style helps people build specific thinking skills, such as the following:

- Thinking independently without undue influence of others
- Clarifying issues or beliefs

- Evaluating information and seeing potential holes
- Minimizing group think

Making the Best Use of Thinking Styles

Now that you understand your preferred thinking styles, let's look at how they play out in your daily life. Write down a situation you have experienced recently (e.g., a decision you needed to make or a problem you solved at work/home).

Situation:

Which styles did you use in this situation?

How did they help you accomplish your goal?

Were there styles that you could have used, but didn't?

These questions are intended to help you become more aware of how you are currently using your thinking styles. If your top style is analytical and your bottom style is systematic, you are likely to approach situations by looking for missing details and inconsistencies, but less likely to begin by putting the situation into a larger context. Knowing your preferences helps you use your strengths more effectively and become more aware of things that you might miss.

Consider the value of each style as you practice your critical thinking skills (see Figure 3.1). For example, a systematic style, the tendency to see the big picture and anticipate consequences, is particularly helpful when you are trying to evaluate information and draw conclusions. A timely style helps you bring a plan of action to life.

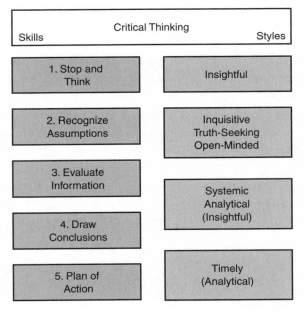

Source: Pearson

Figure 3.1 Consider the value of each style as you practice your critical thinking skills.

Summary

You've explored several positive thinking styles that support skill development and good thinking. Hopefully, you visited the Web site and have a better feel for your own thinking style or styles. When you have done so, you will know more about your own tendencies, the styles you use more frequently, and those you use less frequently. You can also hone and improve your thinking skills. The key lesson here is about being intentional, and the key piece of advice you can take with you is to know your style and grow with your style. It's easier to build your thinking skills when you use your preferred style. You no doubt recognize that some thinking skills will require more work to develop because they don't match your preferred style. At some point, it will be valuable for you to take a tough look at your least preferred styles and work on improving those, but that should come after you build a solid base of skills.

Change Your Thinking... Transform Your Life

Amenah is now back with her family in Iraq, a healthy, growing young girl with every chance to live a full and happy life. That miracle is over. But there are plenty of other miracles needing to happen in the world, dreams to fulfill, and lives to improve. You can be at the heart of all that.

The end of her moving story is the opportunity for the beginning of yours, which brings us back to the subtitle of this book: *Change Your Thinking... Transform Your Life.* You have an opportunity now to commit to a practice of highly effective thinking—and in doing so, you will open yourself up to the potential for greatness.

Like the heroes of "Amenah's Story," you can position yourself to succeed. In the chaotic world today, high-quality critical thinkers can navigate a turbulent global economy, shape a new vision for the education of tomorrow, and lead with wisdom and compassion. You need these skills to think on a world stage, but you also need these skills in your local community, in your neighborhood, and in your home.

You will know that you are making progress when you notice yourself behaving in new and more effective ways, particularly in situations that used to be a challenge for you. People and situations that used to hijack your emotions will no longer have power over you. Opportunities that you didn't know existed or that you didn't know you were looking for will find you. Doors will start to open for you—that you didn't know were there—and you will start walking through them to a richer life.

The people who helped Amenah were, in many ways, people just like you—soldiers and civilians, all volunteers with compassion in their hearts and commitment to a better world in their sights, and they engaged in high-caliber thinking to accomplish an extraordinary feat. Every single person played a critical role; every single person made the crucial difference, a well-thought-out behavior or sound decision that tipped the scale toward success. You too can be the person who tips the scale in a positive direction; you just need to be ready, willing, and prepared.

Getting Started

What we're talking about is *critical thinking*. By *critical*, we don't mean for you to go around criticizing—especially yourself. In fact, critical thinking is quite the opposite. It means you want to understand more fully all the aspects and perspectives of people or ideas, not so you can judge and find fault but rather so you can evaluate more clearly and see the big picture and assess the value in something. You cast a curious and critical eye as you look at any individual or situation, whether it's to consider a relationship or someone who wants to sell you part of a time-share condo.

Now, here is the really huge thing you can take away, in addition to knowing Amenah is doing fine now—*critical thinking is all about you taking charge of your own thinking and owning your life.* Totally! Think about that for a moment. That's a big difference for many people. You've seen people who plod along and see what their mind comes up with next. Or worse, you've seen the ones who turn to others for their opinions, as if they're not even able to think on their own at all. This one key aspect is empowering for you. You can own this enhanced power. You might suppose that you think pretty well so far, but consider what it can mean to develop your own criteria and standards for analyzing and assessing all manner of people and situations.

That's what we're up to here: getting you the tools and the techniques and getting you started in the right direction to improve the quality of the way you examine and think about anything. Like starting a health-fitness regime or personal diet, there are things you can do every day to stretch, exercise, and get better. What follows is a practical daily practice for developing yourself as a great thinker. You will immediately start to experience benefits from using and following this guide. It all starts with you.

My Thinking Styles

If you have not already done so, go to www.ThinkWatson.com/mythinkingstyles and take your free *My Thinking Styles* assessment and learn about the strengths and opportunities embedded in your current thinking style.

Think about your personal style as you review each of the techniques and checklists.

My Thinking Styles	Descriptions
Analytical	Clear thinking, orderly, and rational
Inquisitive	Curious, alert, and interested in the surrounding world
Insightful	Prudent, humble, reflective, and strategic
Open minded	Intellectually tolerant and fair minded
Systematic	Conceptual, process oriented, and intuitive
Timely	Efficient, reliable, and responsive
Truth seeking	Independent, tough minded, and skeptical

Source: Pearson

Figure 4.1   An overview of the various thinking styles discussed in Chapter 3, "Take Stock of Your Style." Remember, you might have a mix of several of these, and you might have some areas where you'd like to grow stronger.

Use This Checklist to Improve Your Thinking

You can start right now building your toolbox of tips, tools, and techniques. Let's start with a look again at the five steps in Figure 4.2, and then advance as you examine "Tips for the Five Steps to Develop Your Thinking Skills NOW."

The following section includes a checklist of key questions to ask yourself the next time you need to make a decision to embrace an opportunity or solve a problem. You might find that the act of making notes in a diary or little black book really supports the practice of each of these.

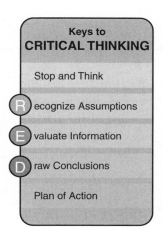

Source: Pearson

Figure 4.2 These are the steps. If it helps you to remember the three action steps in the middle by the acronym RED, all the better. The important thing is to employ these steps in all you do.

Tips for the Five Steps to Develop Your Thinking Skills NOW

The following are suggestions and techniques to help you develop your personal thinking style.

Stop and Think

- What is the situation?
- Is this situation a high priority/high risk or can it wait?

- When does a decision need to be made?
- What are you trying to accomplish?

Ideally, when you are in the "stop and think" step, you want to respond to a situation and not just react. Major Kevin Jarrard, eager to do something about a two-year-old who turned blue and was going to die, stopped to think first. Captain John Nadeau stopped and thought. Lieutenant Colonel David Bellon did. Even Janet Jarrard, rushed the most for time, stopped to consider, "How am I going to do this?" To help you move from reacting to responding, try the following:

1. Do not make decisions when you are emotional or upset. Your feelings will override your logic and could negatively impact your thinking. Before you make a gesture to that road rage driver you'll regret when you learn he's a seven-foot-tall martial arts instructor, consider the consequences. Even if the emotion is positive, like love, give yourself time to be objective about what might affect you for the rest of your life.

2. If you are emotional, upset, or simply not on your "A" game, stall for time. Try pausing for 90 seconds or counting to 10 before you respond. If you can, get some space or take a walk. A change in the scenery can have a tremendous impact on your ability to think through a situation. Hesitate before you send that stinging e-mail at work. Think about the long-term need to get along with your fellow workers.

3. Confirm that you need to make a decision now. Sometimes there can be a sense of urgency around issues (driven by others) that can wait a day to be answered. It is all too easy to

have our lives consumed by urgent trivialities. If this is the case, then say, "Let me think about this," and provide a specific date and time that you will respond to their request. This technique allows you some space and time to think and lets the other party know when they can expect an answer. Although there is an obvious time urgency difference between responding to a proposal and a situation like "What to do? The house is on fire," there are also situations like buying a car where the salesperson will push you to sign immediately. Do you really need a new car? Can you afford this one? Is there more you can find out about this make and model? Yes, there is. Stop and think.

4. If you immediately dismiss another's viewpoint or have an immediate negative response, take note. You could be biased, and it could be impacting your judgment about the issue. If a friend's political leanings are different from yours, that doesn't mean you shouldn't listen to the issues discussed in an election. A critical thinker wants to know all sides and aspects of everything. Who knows, you might find there is merit you would have missed.

5. Quiet time is key to effective decision making; block out time in your schedule for this (early morning/late evening) where you won't be disrupted. Recall Kevin Jarrard kneeling beside his cot. You might find a walk in the park helps you consider best. Even that time you spend in bed before you fall asleep might prove an invaluable time to contemplate all you've absorbed in the day.

Recognize Assumptions

- What do you know? What don't you know?

- What are the unstated assumptions associated with the goal, problem, or information that you know?

- What are your own beliefs that could lead you to passively agree with information without checking the facts?

As it turned out, there was a whole lot of complexity to the task of taking a little Muslim girl and her mother out of Iraq for an operation in the States. Who knew? Would the Christians of America embrace the plight of a child of another religion for her own sake? But consider the way people like Jonathan Malloch considered all he "could know," then sought to develop contingency plans for all he "could not know." Captain Nadeau had friends and influence back at Vanderbilt, but he never assumed getting an operation lined up with a surgeon and the financial help of the hospital was a slam dunk. He reached out and made the right steps to help things happen, or they would not have happened.

1. Identify the key question that you are trying to answer so that you can clarify the specific decision that you are trying to make and any assumptions that you might have around your thinking. Let's say you want to buy a house, or pick out a college to attend. You might assume the home is in a neighborhood you'd fit into, or that the college is the right one for you based on the limited amount you've heard. A lot of things can go with a house bought with a 30-year note, and it might turn out some other school has a far better program in the area in which you decide to specialize.

2. Make a list of your assumptions. This is not only helpful for clarifying your assumptions, but is also helpful after you make a decision to explain why you made a certain decision. Let's say you're considering a prospective spouse, and the fourth item on your list is that you assume you share the same values, but then you find you don't, or you have bitter differences about politics or whether to get drapes or venetian blinds. Explore, explore.

3. Once you know what question you are trying to answer, try to understand the why behind the why. This is sometimes referred to as "the five whys" or the "question behind the question." Write out your question. Then, ask five "whys" to help you identify the root issue to be addressed. Remember as you read this Q&A that it is so easy in a busy world to forget some thoughtful things we actually did do:

   a. Why is the payment for your credit card bill late?
   The bill is late because I didn't receive a paper bill in the mail.

   b. Why didn't you receive a paper bill?
   I wanted to cut down on physical mail and I signed up for online billing. (Oops—I forgot I'd done this.)

   c. Why didn't you receive an online bill?
   Now I remember, I did receive an online bill, but I thought that I had set up auto payments.

   d. Why didn't the auto payments work?
   They didn't work because it turns out that the debit card information was incorrect.

   e. Why was the debit card information incorrect?
   A new debit card had been sent to me with a new expiration date and I forgot to update the account.

In this scenario, we could have focused on the simple question of "why is my credit card late," but the real problem was that the debit card information needed to be updated on the auto payment site. If we had not moved beyond the first question, we would have most likely ended up with a late bill next month, too!

4. Check your understanding with people close to a situation; use active listening to make sure that you understand the situation. Lieutenant Colonel Bellon is a good model here. How could he tell if Kevin Jarrard was "on his game" or thinking up something wacky that could go horribly wrong? He listened, he weighed, and he realized Kevin had given his idea careful thought and even debated it with Captain Nadeau.

5. Identify what you know and what you don't know. Prioritize what you still need to know so that you don't waste time researching what you already know. Being overwhelmed by data is one of the biggest obstacles to making a decision. Also, prioritize what you need to know to make a decision versus what is interesting. Research, especially Internet research, can eat up a lot of valuable time quickly. Let's say you seek to find a reliable contractor. Which reviews do you trust? And why? Don't get lured off on colorful displays of fittings or materials when your target issue is, "Who can best do this?"

Evaluate Information

- What are the alternatives to explore?
- Is your information from credible sources?
- Is your information relevant?

- Is your information accurate?

- Are you being objective?

Janet Jarrard was a PR specialist, yet she couldn't mount a campaign to gather funds because that could have jeopardized the lives of Amenah and her mother. What other ways could she reach out to people for financial and technical help?

Jonathan Malloch examined one alternative scenario where the extraction team would try to take mother and daughter out through Israel instead of Jordan. The information he got wasn't reliable enough to depend upon. He also heard there was an effort to keep the mission of getting Amenah to the States from happening, and Kevin Jarrard was able to help dismiss that as unreliable. But they examined everything. Here's how:

1. Create a process to help you evaluate options. A few ideas include the following:

   a. Determine criteria for making a decision; this will enable you to focus and prioritize on what is most important, generate alternatives, and use criteria to evaluate them.

   b. Make a list of the pros and cons for each option.

   c. Ask...if we do this, then...

   d. Analyze issues from multiple perspectives.

   e. List it out, talk it out, and map it out. Different strategies work for different people; find out what works for you.

2. Play personal devil's advocate—list five reasons against your idea. What are potential flaws to your reasoning? Check with others. Do they see any flaws?

3. When evaluating the best decision, make sure to continually go back to the key question that you are trying to answer. It will keep you focused on the key problem that you are trying to answer.

4. Look at alternatives and allow for creative brainstorming. Crazy ideas can result in some of the best ideas.

5. Make sure that the evidence supports your conclusion and if the evidence doesn't fit your conclusion, don't try to make it fit.

Draw Conclusions

- Ask yourself: Is anything missing? Are there other alternatives that I might have missed?

- Clarify your criteria for evaluation and identify if any of the alternatives can be eliminated.

- Which alternative best matches the success criteria?

For Amenah to successfully come to America, get operated on, and return to Iraq, think how many different people thought through every step multiple times. Jonathan Malloch had to be ready to pull the plug on his colleagues helping if he felt their lives might be at risk. Kevin Jarrard had to keep up his patrols on the Euphrates by pondering all the possible steps that could go right or wrong, and what he could do to help in each instance. Lieutenant Colonel Bellon had to ensure the mission's fit was right for all Marines up and down the command from him.

1. Evaluate different conclusions. Sometimes we can sell ourselves on a solution because it seems to be the best, but we forget to evaluate other options. Identify other possible solutions and evaluate them based upon your established criteria.

2. What are the implications of your decision? Every decision will have consequences, often unintended; you can't anticipate everything, but try to identify what you can anticipate.

3. Ask yourself, is this decision workable? If not, what can you do to make it happen? We can have great ideas, but they are simply ideas if you can't execute on those ideas.

4. Think about what you will feel like if you make the decision that you are considering. How will you feel if you had to explain to someone your rationale for making the decision? Does it still feel like a wise decision? If not, why?

5. What is the time frame for completing the decision? Try to create a reasonable deadline, even if there isn't one imposed by others. This will help to drive you to action. However, remember that some decisions take time. It is important to be patient with the process. We live in a world where we want all of the answers yesterday. Recognize that some decisions can wait and act accordingly.

Plan of Action

- What are the consequences of this decision?

- What plans need to be made to implement this decision?

- What types of resources are needed to implement this decision?

Lieutenant Colonel Bellon had to consider what resources could be expended, what the consequences would be if Amenah died while across the ocean, and if the task was in the spirit of the mission in Iraq at that moment. Doctors Christian and Doyle, aside from knowing who was going to pay for the operation, had the bigger quality-of-life question about what best to do in handling a little body that had more complex issues than expected. What procedure would give her the best chances of long-term survival when going back to a country where she was not likely to get follow-up care nor would there be facilities for additional surgeries if they should be needed?

1. Identify the sequence of steps for implementation and make it happen.

2. What will you do if your decision doesn't work out as planned? What are your contingency plans? List possible problems and potential solutions to help create a contingency plan. Recall how Glenn Susskind and Gary White had a Plan A, Plan B, and even Plan C for almost every possible challenge or obstacle they might face.

3. Clear, open, and frequent communication is necessary when informing others about your decision. When possible, offer more information so that you can ease the concerns or anxiety of others who might be impacted by your decision.

4. Encourage others to share their opinions on your decision. By being open to the ideas of others, you can establish buy-in and help anticipate possible consequences and obstacles that you might have missed. Think of Major Mark A. Lamelza here. He pushed back when David Bellon wanted to support Kevin Jarrard's mission. That's exactly the kind of officer Bellon wanted. Not a yes-man, but one who could

look at all sides and risks. Corporations want that sort of person too.

5. After you implement a decision, evaluate what happens—did you have enough information; were there things you missed? If it was a good decision, why was the decision good?

Don't worry about making mistakes because you are going to make them. The good news from our interviews with some of the world's most enduringly successful people is this: They make a lot of mistakes—more than you and I. The difference is they recognize their mistakes quickly and apply critical thinking skills to learn useful lessons, which they quickly put to work. You can do this too and build a better life for yourself, family, and friends.

Let Yourself Experience Success

What will success look like for you? Ask yourself questions and let the answer or answers evolve. It helps to practice visualizing what it might look like *for you*. We added the emphasis here because it needs to be yours, not borrowed or handed down from the outside world. It has to be yours. You have to own it and critical thinking can do this for you. Make notes to yourself. Success might include material or economic gain. For example, our research shows that critical thinking is associated with higher occupational attainment. Good critical thinkers tend to successfully climb the corporate ladder—and receive the financial rewards that go with that rise. Good critical thinkers are also viewed in the workplace with respect for their ability to use sound judgment, solve problems, and make good decisions, and often for their creativity. So in the career world, critical thinking is tied to reward and respect. However, this is not all there is to it.

Success also includes a number of the qualities shared by the people who participated in "Amenah's Story." They were effective thinkers who possessed a quiet confidence, one that comes from knowing that you have the ability to successfully make something happen. They were genuinely humble about what they were doing, but they were also very sure of their capabilities. David Bellon brought this point home: "At no point did we ever think we were doing something extraordinary. I'll speak for everybody when I say this: We thought we were doing what we were supposed to do. Never once did we sit back and go, holy cow, we're hitting it out of the park with this one! You know our job was to get out there and find a way to make a bad situation better, and this was an opportunity, and we thought this was what we were supposed to do." Perhaps the biggest benefit of having good thinking skills is the self-assurance that comes with the ability to think through even the toughest situations and make the right decisions. It is a can-do attitude, a sense of control and confidence, which is priceless.

Summary

Adopting a new way of thinking will change your life by helping you to see opportunities more clearly, sort through ambiguity more effectively, and make better decisions. Start practicing your new way of thinking today and enjoy greater clarity, confidence, success, and satisfaction. As you change your thinking, you will transform your life.

How can you actually do this? Well, it's pretty much the same sort of behavior shift you'd make when committing to a nutrition or exercise regime. You keep the vision of the "new and improved" you in mind every day, as you keep active toward that goal. So here we go with the tips, tools, and techniques cliff notes:

- Break yourself from the patterns of your past by looking each day at the lives of those around you and in the media, for examples of those who exhibit highly effective thinking—not just the Nobel Prize winners, but those who excel at whatever they set out to do.

- Keep track of your progress in a journal, diary, or a computer file. You'll soon know more and more about you and your thinking style, or styles. Are you improving, stretching yourself to use styles you formerly did not? Are you meeting challenges with more confidence? Are you better prepared for anything? The most effective people in the world develop their own measurement system to track their daily progress. Think of this as having "mini" goals. The strategy is to think-act-measure-correct-improve. This might seem like a lot of work—and it is, at first. However, you will immediately start being more comfortable in your own skin knowing you are becoming the best you can be.

- Keep your mind active. Test yourself with exercises or quizzes. There are numerous thinking challenges on the Internet and, if you look with your now-more-enlightened mind, in the real world around you. How can you be more innovative at work? Is there a better way to approach a particular problem in a more timely or open-minded way? You might find yourself coming up with new revenue streams at work or better ways to balance your personal and professional life. You might fix your finances. And, research indicates that those with active minds live fuller and richer lives the older they get.

■ Reward yourself when you discover you are using thinking powers you may have never thought you had. You can be your own best coach or cheerleader once you start measuring improvement. It's about a better life, so treat yourself right. You will have earned it!

Go forth and matter!

Characters

Major Kevin Jarrard, Commanding Officer, Company L, 3rd Battalion, 23rd Marines. Kevin, Kelly, Caleb, Hannah, Rachel, Ethan at Riverside Military Academy where Kevin is currently serving as the Commandant of Cadets.

Source: Kevin Jarrard

Captain John Nadeau, a Navy reservist in his sixties, a professor at Vanderbilt University School of Medicine. Dr. John Nadeau was a top hypertension specialist at Vanderbilt on his second tour of duty as a battlefield surgeon with the U.S. Marine Corps in Haditha, Iraq.

Source: Marines—Mark Lamelza

Lieutenant Colonel David G. Bellon, Commanding Officer, 3rd Battalion, 23rd Marines, 4th Marine Division. He is now a colonel in the reserves having deployed three times to Iraq and once to Afghanistan. He now lives in St. Louis, Missouri, with his wife and kids and works in international trade.

Source: David Bellon

Major Mark A. Lamelza, Operations Officer, 3rd Battalion, 23rd Marines, 4th Marine Division. Mark Lamelza is pictured with his wife Jennifer and daughter Jade on vacation in Naples, Florida. Mark and his family live in Nashville, Tennessee. Mark works for the professional services organization Deloitte as an Information Technology Manager. Mark is still in the reserves and he now commands 3rd Battalion, 23rd Marines as a Lieutenant Colonel.

Source: Marines—Mark Lamelza

Major Kevin E. Clark, Executive Officer, who shared an office with Mark Lamelza.

Major Jake Falcone, Battalion Communications Officer, facilitated clearance for Amenah and her mother to enter the United States through the State Department and Department of Homeland Security. Jake Falcone is pictured with his wife Clare and children Katherine and Joseph. Jake works for CACI as a government contractor in the Washington, D.C., area. Jake is still serving in the Marine Reserves as a Major aboard Marine Corps Base Quantico, Virginia.

Source: Jake Falcone

Colonel H. Stacy Clardy III, now a Brigadier General, came to Haditha for a visit. Kevin, with Lieutenant Colonel Bellon's permission, told Colonel Clardy what he was up to and said, "Sir, if this all lines up, would you provide us a helicopter?" Though skeptical, the colonel said that if everything else came together that the regiment would provide a helicoptor.

Sergeant Bryan C. Velasquez, a Company Lima squad leader, 3rd Battalion, 23rd Marine Regiment, Regimental Combat Team 5, who discovered Amenah on a routine patrol through the city. She appeared to be a normal little girl, except for her blue lips and fingers.

Amenah al-Bayati, two-year-old Haditha girl.

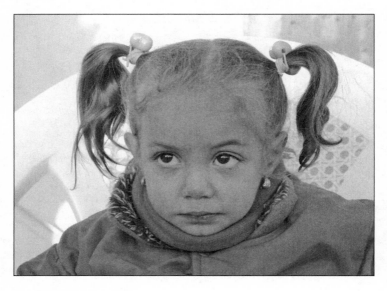

Source: Marines—Mark Lamelza

Alaa Thabit Fatah, father. "Perhaps he was involved in the insurgency, perhaps he wasn't," Major Jarrard said. "It's difficult to tell from the reports we have. But as far as I'm concerned, he's my friend."

Source: Marines—Mark Lamelza

Maha Muhammad Bandar, mother (41-year-old).

Source: Marines—Mark Lamelza

Sheik Said Flayah Othman, tribal chief who gave the okay; from the al-Jughayfi tribe.

Dr. Karla Christian, M.D., pediatric heart surgeon and an associate professor of cardiology at Vanderbilt. (Amenah returned to Haditha March 7 after undergoing open heart surgery at the Monroe Carell Jr. Children's Hospital at Vanderbilt University in Nashville, Tennessee.)

Dr. Thomas Doyle, M.D., a pediatric cardiologist at Monroe Carell Jr. Children's Hospital at Vanderbilt University.

Kevin Churchwell, M.D., the CEO of the Monroe Carell Jr. Children's Hospital at Vanderbilt University.

Samir Sumaidaie, Iraqi ambassador to the United States, also from Haditha.

Janet Jarrard, Major Kevin Jarrard's aunt, who helped line up details to get the mother and daughter to the States. She and Kelly Jarrard, Kevin's wife, helped raise money. She is semiretired and lives in Franklin, Tennessee, where she spends most of her time with her two young grandsons. Chief among her charitable endeavors is the John Jarrard Foundation, established in 2001 to honor her late husband, which has raised over $800,000 for various charitable organizations in his home state of Georgia.

Source: Janet Jarrard

Jonathan Malloch, Jonathan not only had a medical background, an EMT background, and had worked for FEMA, but he also did emergency medical management whenever he was called on to do it. He had extensive military connections and a military background. He orchestrated the extraction team.

Lisa Van Wye, R.N., Janet Jarrard's friend, a nurse in Bowling Green, Kentucky. Janet asked Lisa to fly with the extraction team to Jordan because they had to have a woman on the team escorting Amenah and her mom.

Deanna Dolan, with World Relief, which provided an Arabic interpreter, cultural orientation, and helped with planning culturally appropriate food.

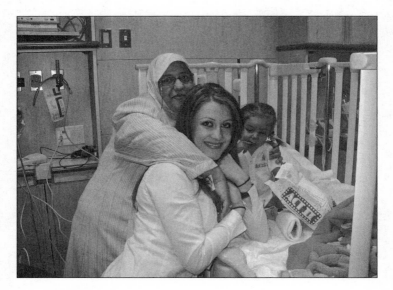

Source: Deanna Dolan

Pastor Steve and Sarah Berger, Grace Chapel Church in Lieper's Fork, Tennessee. They let Amenah and her mother, as well as Deanna Dolan and the interpreter, stay at their home. Steve and Sarah continue their work at Grace Chapel. Since their son, Josiah, went to Heaven in August 2009, they have written a book and have committed themselves to teaching people how to have a biblical perspective when a loved one passes on. They can be reached through www.gracechapel.net and http://haveheart.net.

Source: Deanna Dolan

Robin Smith, a family friend and an executive with the BB&T Bank in Gainesville, Georgia, Kevin Jarrard's hometown.

Glenn Susskind, medic, member of the extraction team.

Gary White, member of the extraction team.

Blackwater Worldwide, now known as Xe Services LLC, is a private military company founded as Blackwater USA in 1997 by Erik Prince, a former Navy Seal with inherited wealth, and Al Clark. Blackwater was often contracted to guard U.S. diplomats, an activity that led to the company becoming embroiled in controversy, particularly for its activities in Iraq. In October 2007, Blackwater USA was renamed Blackwater Worldwide. It announced on February 13, 2009, that it would operate under the new name "Xe." In a memo sent to employees, President Gary Jackson wrote that the new name "reflects the change in company focus away from the business of providing private security." The company was purchased on December 17, 2010, by USTC Holdings, an investment group.

Travel note: Commercial flights were paid for by donations except a Sikorsy CH-53 helicopter to take the family and Kevin to the Jordan border and the family's return to Al Asad Airbase in Al Anbar Province, where they boarded an MV-22 Osprey for the final leg of the voyage to Haditha.

Cognitive Biases: Common Mental Mind Traps

Mind traps are like optical illusions that fool you into thinking you're right when you're not. It is important to get a proper introduction to these mental mistakes because you will run into them as you practice a new way of thinking. Social scientists have identified many different kinds of mental mistakes associated with the way human beings process information. The pioneering work of Amos Tversky and Daniel Kahneman, culminating in Kahneman being awarded the Nobel Prize in 2002 for economic sciences, sheds light on the human tendency to make systematic errors in certain situations.

Basically, humans use simple rules, heuristics, to make judgments. Although heuristics are quite useful, they operate like shortcuts that save us time, but they also create systematic errors. A few of the more prevalent ones are described here. They are grouped so that you can see which of the five steps of critical thinking they are most likely to impact.

Grabbing Glory and Pushing Blame (Step 2: Recognize Assumptions)

- A **fundamental attribution error** is an error in attributing cause. If someone makes a mistake, there is a tendency to attribute the mistake to the individual's personality rather than the situation. For example, if someone makes a mistake at work, the cause will more likely be attributed to a personal shortcoming than work overload or time pressure. Not really fair, is it? This trap leads to faulty assumptions and poorly defined problems that skew a situation in the wrong direction from the start. To minimize this error, analyze the situation by asking questions about the environment and its impact.

- **Self-serving bias** is the tendency to make assumptions about what is fair or right in a way that favors our own self-interest. For example, if you ask four people how much (what percentage) they contributed to a project, the number will exceed 100 percent. We tend to take more than our fair share of credit. When information is ambiguous, we tend to interpret it in a way that benefits our self-interest. To minimize this error, pay particular attention to the contributions of others, and recognize that you might be underestimating their time and value, relative to your own. An open-minded style will help you become more aware of the contributions of others.

Asking the Wrong Questions (Step 3: Evaluate Information)

■ **Confirmation bias** is the tendency to search for information that confirms your beliefs. If you are responsible for making important decisions, underline this mind trap and keep it squarely in your view because this trap snaps on a regular basis and you don't want to make a crucial decision with lopsided information. To minimize this bias, ask yourself, "Am I being objective?" and actively seek out people who will articulate a contrary view. Look for people with inquisitive and truth-seeking styles who can help you explore all sides of a position.

■ **Anchoring** is the tendency to give undue weight to the first information you receive. Hammond, Keeney, and Raiffa[1] asked people two questions that we invite you to answer:

  ■ Is the population of Turkey greater than 35 million?

  ■ What is your best estimate of Turkey's population?

They found that information in the first question, specifically the figure 35 million, influenced the answers to the second question. When they used 100 million in the first question, peoples' estimates to the second question were much larger. The information anchored how they thought about the question. As you can imagine, anchoring is used as a negotiation technique, so be aware of how initial numbers and information can impact the way you evaluate subsequent information.

- The **framing effect** occurs when a person's response changes based on the way the question is framed. Consider the example we mentioned previously: You need surgery and your doctor says to you, "92% of the patients survive surgery." That sounds positive. Now let's say the doctor says, "8% of the patients die in surgery." That doesn't sound as good, and people are more likely to reject the latter statement. The same odds of survival, but different acceptance due to the way the information is framed. When you gather information, look at the frame because it could unduly influence your decision. You want to focus on the information (e.g., odds of survival), not the way it is framed.

- **Group think** occurs when members of a tightly knit group try to minimize conflict and reach consensus without critically testing, analyzing, and evaluating ideas. The Kennedy administration's decision to invade Cuba (Bay of Pigs) and the George W. Bush administration's decision to invade Iraq have both been described as examples of group think. The ingredients for group think include an inner circle of advisors who are closely aligned and the absence of someone who holds an alternative viewpoint or plays devil's advocate. A truth-seeking style is particularly valuable for surfacing the tough, but necessary questions.

Curious Conclusions (Step 4: Draw Conclusions)

- **Optimism bias** is the tendency to overestimate positive outcomes and underestimate negative outcomes. This bias is a double-edged sword because optimism is an admirable quality associated with being resilient, but underestimating risk is dangerous. The best safeguard against this mind trap is good planning. Everyone in "Amenah's Story" maintained a positive attitude, but their plans were meticulous and they recognized and accepted that a single glitch could stop the project.

- **Planning fallacy** is the tendency to underestimate the time, costs, and risks of future actions and, at the same time, overestimate the benefits of those same actions. Think about the last project at work that was late, had cost overruns, and fell short of expectations. It probably didn't take you long to come up with an example because this mental mistake occurs frequently. To counter this fallacy, leverage timely and analytical thinking styles as you prepare to make a decision.

- **Sunk cost** fallacy is also common and occurs when we make a decision in a way that justifies a past decision. It is reminiscent of the catch phrase "throwing good money after bad." Sunk cost comes from economics where the past investment (of time or money) can't be recovered and should be irrelevant to the present decision, but research shows that it is not. If you have already invested in a project or relationship, you are likely to hang on and want to make it work because of your past involvement rather than your analysis of the future success. To minimize this bias, you need to do an emotional temperature check and bring feelings (e.g., regret, fear of failure) to the surface, so you can more readily assess their influence. Then, shift your attention to an analysis of the current and future investments required and the likely return on investment.

Endnote

1. Hammond, John S., Ralph L. Keeney, and Howard Raiffa. 1998. *Smart Choices: A Practical Guide to Making Better Decisions.* Harvard Business School.

Resources

Congratulations! You have made it to the end of this book and the beginning of a new, or perhaps renewed, approach to improve your thinking, and that is a great accomplishment. This appendix provides suggested readings and additional resources to support your thinking success.

Online Resources and Social Media

Blogs

Critical Thinkers

URL: www.critical-thinkers.com

Authors: Chad Fife, Breanne Harris, Heather Ishikawa, and Elizabeth Pauker

Good decision making and innovative thinking are coveted competencies in today's world, but how do you develop the underlying skills? Through improved critical thinking, of course! Critical-thinkers.com guides you through the essentials of critical thinking,

Pearson's RED critical thinking model, and how to think critically in real life and in your job.

Critical Thinking in the Real World
URL: http://janethinz.com
Author: Janet Hinz

Learn about hot topics and the critical thinking necessary to address them through this blog and accompanying radio show.

3C Pearson Learning Solutions
URL: http://www.pearsoncustom.com/professional/blog
Authors: Amy Rondinel and Sean Stowers

Follow key trends and topics in professional education and workplace skill development, including critical thinking. The primary focus is on executive development, online and blended learning, certification, and innovation in education.

Assessment Buzz
URL: www.AssessmentBuzz.com
Author: Breanne Harris

Engage in an interactive discussion about the use of assessments for personal and organizational development. This blog includes critical thinking topics and how to assess both thinking and personality.

eBook

Critical Thinking eBook

URL: www.ThinkWatson.com/ebook

Author: Chad Fife and Scott Flander

Learn how the RED model helps you make good decisions and the five reasons to train employees to think critically. This eBook is aimed at professional development audiences.

Facebook Groups

Critical Thinkers Facebook Group

URL: http://facebook.com/criticalthinkers

Connect and network with others who are interested in critical thinking. You can also check out the critical thinking groups on LinkedIn by searching "critical thinking in business."

Now You're Thinking Facebook Group

URL: http://www.facebook.com/NowYoureThinking

Participate in the Now You're Thinking Facebook Group and share information about *Now You're Thinking* and additional resources available for continued learning.

Videos

Critical Thinking: No Longer Just a C-Suite Skill (Video)

URL: http://www.youtube.com/talentlens

Author: Ed Reilly, CEO, American Management Association

Business has changed and critical thinking and agility is required at all levels of the organization as decisions get pushed downstream. Learn how you can be prepared for the emerging workplace.

Critical Thinking: Today's #1 Skill (Video)

URL: http://www.youtube.com/talentlens

Consultants and HR professionals discuss real-world critical thinking, why it's today's top workplace skill, and how to assess candidates with the Watson-Glaser™ II Critical Thinking Appraisal.

Critical Thinking Video via YouTube

URL: http://www.youtube.com (Search for "critical thinking Qualia Soup")

Created by: Qualia Soup

Listen to a clear and concise overview of critical thinking and how it works in our lives.

Essential Skills for 21st Century Workplace (Webcast)

URL: www.amanet.org (Search for "essential skills for 21st century workplace webcast")

Authors: Edward Reilly, CEO, American Management Association; Ken Kay, President, Partnership for 21st Century Skills; and Charlie Kreitzberg, CEO, Cognetics Corporation

Learn the key skills students and employees need to be successful in the twenty-first century workplace. The importance of critical thinking in the twenty-first century workplace is also highlighted.

Increasing Critical Thinking in the Workplace: The Raw Material of 21st Century Success (Webcast)

URL: www.hr.com (Search for "increasing critical thinking in the workplace")

Author: Judy Chartrand, Consulting Chief Scientist, Pearson TalentLens; presented by HR.com

The Department of Labor identified critical thinking as the raw material that underlies fundamental workplace competencies, such as problem solving, decision making, planning, and risk management. Learn how to assess critical thinking skills and how to build those skills in the workplace.

Articles

Critical Thinking Means Business whitepaper

URL: http://thinkwatson.com/whitepaper

Authors: Judy Chartrand, Heather Ishikawa, and Scott Flander

Learn to apply and develop the NEW #1 workplace skill using the RED model of critical thinking. This paper describes critical thinking solutions for increasing organizational effectiveness, including a model for understanding and developing critical thinking. It also provides trainers with some specific techniques for developing critical thinking that can jump-start the process.

HR Executive—Thinking Critically

URL: http://www.hreonline.com (Search for "critical thinking")

Success in today's tight economy is defined by making the right decisions, solving the problems that truly impede success, and anticipating the trends that are redefining the competitive landscape. Learn how selecting good critical thinkers will set a new bar for your organization's performance.

Trends in Executive Development Survey (research)

URL: http://www.leadershipdevelopmenttrends.com

Authors: Bonnie Hageman, CEO Executive Development Associates, and Judy Chartrand, Consulting Chief Scientist, Pearson TalentLens

Gain insight into the best practices, emerging needs, top priorities, and cutting-edge approaches to leadership and executive development. This longitudinal research describes how to accelerate the development of emerging leaders, why strategic thinking is a top skill gap and what to do about it, how to accelerate the development of emerging leaders, and what the future of executive development holds.

Harvesting Tomorrow's Leaders: How Do You Recognize Your Top Talent and Groom Them for Leadership Positions?

URL: http://thinkwatson.com/downloads/ Harvesting-Tomorrows-Leaders.pdf

Authors: Jim Bolt, CEO Bolt Consulting, and Bonnie Hagemann, T&D, July 2009

Learn the steps organizations can take to identify and develop their high-potential talent and the signs to look for when someone is about to derail.

Assessments

My Thinking Styles

URL: www.ThinkWatson.com/mythinkingstyles

Do your friends and family want to complete the My Thinking Styles assessment? Invite them to go to this site and complete a brief form of the assessment.

Watson-Glaser™ II Critical Thinking Appraisal

URL: www.ThinkWatson.com

Watson-Glaser™ II is the gold standard for measuring critical thinking and decision-making skills. The assessment is used worldwide by corporations, talent management consulting firms, and schools to select great managers, develop high-potential professionals and future leaders, and admit applicants into challenging programs. Learn how you can use this assessment in your organization.

Books for Professional Development

Successful Manager's Handbook, 7th ed.

Susan Gebelein, Kristie Nelson-Neuhaus, Carol Skube, David Lee, Lisa Stevens, Lowell Hellervik, and Brian Davis. Minneapolis, MN: Personnel Decisions International Corporation, 2004.

ISBN: 093852920

A one-volume library filled with smart, practical ideas and suggestions that you can use immediately on the job. This is the place to turn when you need new ideas, have to get your team up to speed fast, or want to prepare for the next level in your career. The entire first section, Thought Leadership, is devoted to critical thinking.

Successful Executive's Handbook

David Lee, Elaine Sloane, Kristie Nelson-Neuhaus, and Susan Gebelein. Minneapolis, MN: Personnel Decisions International Corporation, 1999.

ISBN: 0972577009

An essential tool for executives—and aspiring executives— whether they lead a *Fortune 500* company or a small organization.

Drawing from more than 30 years of research and work with executives around the world, it provides business-relevant strategies for improving on-the-job performance and mentoring others. The Thinking and Strategic Management chapters address the critical thinking issues encountered by leaders.

FYI: For Your Improvement, A Guide for Development and Coaching, 5th ed.
Michael Lombardo, and Robert Eichinger. Minneapolis, MN: Lominger International, 2009.
ISBN: 9781933578170

An easy-to-use development tool that features a chapter of actionable tips for each of 67 Leadership Architect® competencies, 19 career stallers and stoppers, and 7 global focus areas. The topics that relate to critical thinking include strategic skills, making complex decisions, and creating new and different opportunities.

Awaken, Align, Accelerate: A Guide to Great Leadership
Scott Nelson and Jason Ortmeier. Edina, MN: Beaver's Pond Press, 2010.
ISBN: 9781592983551

A simple, yet powerful framework that invites leaders to embrace the challenge of developing in today's current world. Filled with over 1,500 development suggestions and coaching tips, self-assessments, real-world case studies, and sample development plans, this unique guide is a valuable development asset for any leader. Features several chapters related to critical and strategic thinking.

Michael M. Lombardo (Author)

Visit Amazon's Michael M. Lombardo page and find books, read about the author, and more.

Resources for Students

THINK Critically.

Peter Facione. Englewood Cliffs, NJ: Prentice Hall PTR, 2010.

ISBN: 0205738451

A cutting-edge, self-reflective guide for improving critical thinking skills through careful analysis and thoughtful evaluation of contemporary culture and issues. Taking cues from everyday life—education, business, health sciences, social work, law, government policy issues, and current events—*THINK Critically* bridges the principles of critical thinking with real-world application.

Critical Thinking: Consider the Verdict, 5th ed.

Bruce N. Waller. Englewood Cliffs, NJ: Prentice Hall, 2011.

Organized around lively and authentic examples drawn from jury trials, contemporary political and social debate, and advertising, this introduction shows students how to detect fallacies and how to examine and construct cogent arguments. Accessible and reader friendly—yet thorough and rigorous—it shows how to integrate all logic skills into the critical decision-making process.

Becoming a Better Critical Thinker: A User Friendly Manual,
6th ed.

Sherry Diestler. Englewood Cliffs, NJ: Prentice Hall, 2011.

ISBN: 0132413132

This book trains students to distinguish high-quality, well-supported arguments from arguments with little or no evidence to support them. It develops the skills required to effectively evaluate the many claims facing them as citizens, learners, consumers, and human beings, and also to be effective advocates for their beliefs.

Now You're Thinking about Career Success

Judy Chartrand, Stewart Emery, Russ Hall, Heather Ishikawa, and John Maketa. Upper Saddle River, NJ: Pearson Education, 2011.

Prepare for a successful career. Learn how to use thinking skills to differentiate yourself from other job candidates and give yourself a competitive advantage. Know how to step into the job and perform with confidence by using your thinking skills.

Now You're Thinking about Student Success

Judy Chartrand, Stewart Emery, Russ Hall, Heather Ishikawa, and John Maketa. Upper Saddle River, NJ: Pearson Education, 2011.

Learn how to successfully navigate through school and into a rewarding career. Use a new model for thinking and a series of relevant questions to help you organize your thoughts to meet the challenges of school.

The Re-Discovery of Common Sense: A Guide to Critical Thinking

Chuck Clayton. Bloomington, IN: iUniverse, Inc., 2007.

ISBN: 0595437087

Teach yourself critical thinking skills with this practical guide. You will learn concepts, methods, and resources to make informed decisions, complete tasks quickly and effectively, shop smarter, and create a fun life for yourself.

Critical Thinking Skills Success in 20 Minutes a Day

Lauren Starkey. New York, NY: Learning Express, LLC, 2004.

ISBN: 1576855082

Become an effective critical thinker in just 20 minutes a day! Whether at work, at school, or at home, critical thinking skills are essential for success. Learning to think critically will improve your decision-making and problem-solving skills, giving you the tools you need to tackle the tough decisions and choices you face.

My Thinking Lab

URL: www.MyThinkingLab.com

MyThinkingLab is a series of online courses that accompany Pearson's textbooks. This resource engages students in active learning—it's modular, self-paced, accessible anywhere with Web access, and adaptable to each student's learning style—and instructors can easily customize MyThinkingLab to better meet their students' needs.

Training

Critical Thinking University

Pearson TalentLens

This online learning environment enables participants to develop and apply critical thinking skills in the workplace. The foundation is the three dimensions of the Watson-Glaser™ II Critical Thinking Appraisal (RED). Learners develop their skills through a sequence of interactive activities built around real-world situations. Social learning tools provide self-directed learning, feedback, and coaching. The result is a personalized experience that leads to better problem solving and decision making in an increasingly complex business world.

Length: Training on-demand

Tel: 888.298.6227

URL: http://thinkwatson.com/training-online-training.php

Critical Thinking Boot Camp

Pearson TalentLens/Executive Development Associates

This is an onsite workshop to train employees to think critically. As the "boot camp" name suggests, attendees will be immersed in an intensive, three-phase development process focused on learning practical skills. Each attendee will gain a "Masters-level" understanding of critical thinking and the tools to take their decision making to the next level, with 74 percent reporting they actually apply their new skills on the job.

Length: 2 days

Tel: 888.298.6227

URL: http://thinkwatson.com/training-onsite-training.php

Critical Thinking Seminar #2533

American Management Association

This two-day public workshop provides hands-on experience with a battery of practical tools (including the Watson-Glaser™ II Critical Thinking Appraisal) to help you make critical thinking an indispensable part of your skill set. You'll find out things you didn't know about yourself and make discoveries that can literally change your life. Instead of concentrating on theories, you'll be working with an expert instructor to get comfortable with a concrete set of tools. You'll then be ready to benefit from your new skills immediately when you return to your job.

Length: 2 days

Tel: 877.566.9441

URL: http://www.amanet.org

Advanced Critical Thinking Seminar #2228

American Management Association

This course will give you two full days to practice applying a critical thinking model to the situational challenges you encounter in your own organization. Working through a series of practical cases, you will explore the impact that corporate culture, competing priorities, globalization, technology, and diverse communication styles have on critical thinking. You'll learn strategies and tactics for effectively navigating complex problem solving and decision making and become better prepared to take appropriate action in each situation. Finally, you'll have the opportunity to apply the critical thinking process you've learned to a specific challenge you're facing at work and receive feedback from your instructor and peers to improve your effectiveness.

Length: 2 days

Tel: 877.566.9441

URL: http://www.amanet.org

Index

O

objectivity when evaluating
information, 71-72

open-minded thinking style,
86-88

opinions, separating facts from, 65

optimism bias, 129

Othman, Sheik Said Flayah, 24,
69, 120

overgeneralization, 73

P

personal experience, as source of
assumptions, 64

persuasion, evaluating, 71

plan of action, developing, 76-77,
107, 109

planning fallacy, 129

Prince, Erik, 124

problem solving. *See* thinking
models

Q – R

quiet time, 101

racism, feelings contributing to, 54

*The Re-Discovery of Common
Sense: A Guide to Critical
Thinking,* 142

recognize assumptions (critical
thinking step), mind traps
affecting, 126

RED model of critical thinking, 77

reflective thinking, 60-63, 99, 101

relevancy of information,
evaluating, 68-70

resources for information,
131-144

Rumore, Wayne, 11

S

Sanfey, Alan, 53

self-serving bias, 126

Semir (Iraqi captain), 22

Silsby, Laura, 79-80

Smith, Robin, 16, 124

stated assumptions, unstated
assumptions versus, 65

"stop and think" (reflective
thinking), 60-63, 99, 101

storytelling. *See* Amenah's story

students, resources for
information, 140-142

styles of thinking. *See* thinking
styles

success, experiencing, 109-110

*Successful Executive's
Handbook,* 138

W – Z